Mary,

Happy Birthday!

This is a book my good friend Gim put together for a good cause
I used a pen name but am sure you will easily
find out which is my contribution.
Hope you enjoy the stories of these women!

Warmly,

Eugine

Sushi & Tapas

Life Stories by and of Young Women

Edited by

Pepukaye Bardouille
& Gim Huay Neo

ISBN 978-1-105-05743-4

for Pepukaye's mother, Raj:

teacher, agitator, empath

for Gim's nieces, Sze Min and Yi Teng:

our next generation

3

Foreword

It would be fair to say that we were going through challenging times when 'the book project' was embarked upon. For a start, we were both relocating—literally and figuratively: Gim moved east from New York to Lagos, while Pep headed west from London to Washington D.C.

The project was conceived by Gim one warm April afternoon in 2010, and shared with Pep over a crackling phone line a few weeks later and a continent away. We'd met some months before and apparently both needed to channel the mix of emotions that accompany 'major change' into something at once focused, creative and bigger than ourselves.

In browsing bookshelves, we had felt a dearth of literature that spoke of the experiences of young women, and believed that it could be heartening, interesting and perhaps even inspiring to offer a glimpse into how some in our generation have thought, felt and dealt with life's 'inevitables': men, children, parents, career, fertility, self image, faith, dreams.

Knowing that others had likely been there (wherever "that difficult place" might be) gave us, at the time, an inexplicable semblance of reprieve. Thus, we felt that sharing the stories of those around us could probably provide lessons about the essence of the human condition for others, too.

The idea was to bring together women from around the world in their twenties to forties to share parts of their personal journeys. Our premise was simple: While we are unique beings, there are common denominators in the lives of people everywhere – be they on the surface or hidden underneath – which we can take comfort in and draw inspiration from.

Upon starting this (ad)venture, we told everyone we knew about it. That commits you to the project in the public domain so there'll be no backtracking and no procrastination, we were advised. How very true! From conception to fruition, this baby has taken more than a year to deliver. It would probably have taken us longer if friends and colleagues had not prodded us gently along the way, asking "How's the book coming along" every now and then. For that, we are indebted!

This book has been a blessing on many fronts. Working on it has kept us busy, but has also provided a source of energy, inspiration and renewal. The project has pushed us to juggle schedules and deadlines. It has been a reason to be in touch with one another and our authors across continents and time zones. Editing the stories have put us for a moment in others' shoes. Along the way, we've healed.

Our lessons? That life is as random as it is beautiful! That there is much to learn from the people in our midst. And, as many have witnessed, that the spirit is resilient.

Some of the contributors are friends, former classmates and colleagues. Others are friends of friends or people whose paths we have crossed in the course of an ordinary day. In many cases, we have only met 'virtually', interacting briefly over the phone, exchanging ideas and edits by email. The fact that more than two dozen women came together to create this, we believe, is in part design and in part destiny. To the women who put pen to paper, we are deeply grateful for your belief in this project and for your immense trust and generosity in sharing your stories.

We hope that this book will encourage the reader to take heart in others' experiences and to take pride in who you are, regardless of what life is throwing your way at this point in time. When times are trying, take comfort in knowing that you are far from alone—that someone has been there and come out stronger. And on brighter days, Laugh! Celebrate! Enjoy! We probably don't do it enough.

A final note: Together with the authors, we have pledged all proceeds from the sale of this book to charitable causes that help women and youth. Thank you for your support.

Pepukaye Bardouille   *Gim Huay Neo*

September 2011

Contents

Little Ghost of Change

By Marije Nederveen

Time changes. Times change. We are in constant motion –
our bodies, minds and souls endlessly evolving with our
surroundings – ageing, maturing, travelling. To a limited
extent, we have a hand in shaping this evolution - at times,
we do so with deliberation and at a higher level of
consciousness; perhaps more often than not, we simply go
with the flow and let routines move us along.

I enjoy clinging to memories, meeting old friends and
relishing what has been before. For some reason,
experiences and encounters always taste sweeter as
memories rather than when they are in the moment.

Sometimes, though, I forget that what has been in the past
is not the present, and should not be an expectation of
tomorrow. We have to let go – be it the jubilation of birth
or the pain of a loss. Fading out the past and archiving the
old emotions and thoughts is essential to growth and
renewal as it allows us to think new thoughts and feel new
emotions. Part and parcel of the human experience. - *Ed*

~ 1 ~

She looks back at you or maybe she looks slightly away. Is
it a stern, serious or shy look? I'm still not sure. A bow in her
hair, a dress which falls to her knees, and shoes like I always
wanted, because they make you look like a dancer. A small
bag dangles from her left arm. Is she also carrying a small
hat?

I found this drawing of a little girl on the side of a
pavement in Belgrade, also known as the White City, along
the confluence of the Danube and the Sava rivers. I was on

my way to a museum, but the guard told me in French that I would need to return the next day; it was closing time.

I never made it back, but the trip was worth it: I ran into her. She looked about four, maybe five years old. Like her, I was taught to look up, something I had trouble with when I was her age. I was shy, preferring to look down and promptly blushing whenever anyone addressed me.

But, I was most certainly not such a perfect dresser. My Mom tried her very best – it did not work. I wore similar dresses especially made for me, bows tied in my braided hair and socks pulled up in the morning. All ready for the day.

Somehow, though, the outfit seldom remained in the same shape as evening approached. Socks cheekily slipped down, bows somehow got lost and dresses mysteriously bunched up around my waist, leaving underwear exposed as I stomped my feet through mud and grass. Probably one of the reasons why I was never given those pretty, preppy shoes.

I'm a far cry from that little girl now, but also different from the woman who ran into this image on the pavement just a few months ago.

I was in the White City to take a break, to think and to enjoy a love interest that seemed promising at the time. It started off quite well, but somewhere in the middle we managed to get into an argument. As it goes, I cried, he frowned, then we made up and by the end, contemplated that it could have been different if we had lived closer together, but for now our story ended. All in six days.

Still I enjoyed my stay. The beautiful spring weather, the buzz of the city and the random strangers who would talk to me from time-to-time. One being a man close to his seventies. He said he knew who killed Kennedy and proposed himself as the next presidential candidate who would subsequently ensure the replacement of Serbia's cherished Republic with a monarchy. Much more fascinating than what I really needed to think about and a fabulous reason to dust off my rusty French.

Just before my trip, I had heard that the organisation I was working for was closing down, and then my landlord told me he wanted to sell the apartment I loved. When it rains, it pours. Change had announced itself without my consent, and I wasn't quite sure where to begin dealing with it. Like many women around me, I identify with my job. I really enjoy the work I do and this one had great benefits – travelling to various countries to meet inspiring people, an opportunity to constantly develop my skills and knowledge, and contributing to something I deeply cared about. It was the job I had been dreaming about since I was a little girl. Maybe not as a five-year-old, but certainly the fifteen-year-old who desperately wanted to leave the village where she had been exposing her underwear, much to the embarrassment of her Mom. The question was, did I take with me any other dreams from that village? Perhaps, when I left the White City, I was little further from where I had begun – I had met the little girl. That was a start.

Back home I posted the picture of the little girl on my social networking page. She drew attention. A friend from Georgia asked where she came from and another lady in Fiji decided to use her as her own profile picture. They simply thought it was moving.

Looking at her again, the text beneath the drawing also fascinates me. Maybe it's the name of the artist that drew her, but the letters aren't really clear. Modern technology doesn't provide any answers: the digit followed by one hundred zeroes gives no *Google* search hits on the name, the possible date or the numbers – discounting the hits for window shade sizes of course. Seventy-two could be her height, but then again what does the other one mean? So whatever the artist's intention, he or she already doesn't want a particular credit for it.

And does she represent a real girl? It's like looking at a little ghost. I wondered about it every now and then, but had to leave her again for a while – for one of my travels.

This time to Indonesia. On my day off I found myself at the back of a friend's motorbike. Taking in fumes, sounds and an incredibly diverse group of people humming by on the perpetually congested streets of the vast capital, Jakarta. We were singing some African songs I had picked up long ago and he chanted some of his favourite tunes. My friend has no home of his own. He prefers to live in seven different places, combines Sufi wisdom with prayer at a Catholic church and has energy like no other. We had fun hanging out and went to the old part of the city. Both enjoying our favourite pastimes, me taking pictures, him making people smile and both of us talking to anyone who would listen. We ended up drinking a coke to face the scorching heat, while a guard of the governor's house we had visited shared a ghost story. A white woman had been murdered over a century ago. I think I have forgotten the details of her death due to the heat, but the guards reported seeing her at night sometimes. They even laughed as they said she looked like me. I gave them an even bigger grin back as it reminded me of my own little ghost.

Lightning didn't strike then, but a thought did enter my mind, what a wonderful thing it would be to write a story about this woman, or even better about the little ghost. What a great adventure it would be to find out where she came from, who gave her those watchful eyes that looked straight into the dream I had forgotten about: to write, or better still, to make up stories and share them.

"She looked up from under the table. She had been playing there for a while now... Waiting to go out, but it was taking more time than she wanted. So long. And it already was one of those very long Sundays. They had been talking first about the weather, then about Papa's work and now about something she didn't understand as their voices spoke in a hushed tone. She looked at the ant that was making its way along the table cloth. It was probably aiming for the sugar that had been spilled when added to Aunt Sylvie's tea. Mama was quiet most of the time, but now all of them were silent. She saw how her mother was fumbling with her hands and Papa was tapping his foot. The cat was lying on Aunt Sylvie's lap, being petted feverishly. So much so that he decided to jump off and walk his lazy body out of the kitchen towards the living room.

Freed from the cat, Aunt Sylvie stood up and asked her to come up from under the table. "Shall we go out? I promised you an ice cream right?" She stood up, but felt a bit unsteady on her feet. Her legs had started to sleep since she had been sitting in the same position for so long. "Are you okay?" Aunt Sylvie asked. She nodded. "We will go to the ice-cream parlour and buy you a treat." Aunt Sylvie said.

This awkward conversation seemed directed more towards her mother though than to her, she thought. Her mother's face was a bit strange when she smiled at her and said: "Be careful of your dress." "She's a big girl, she will be fine Anna," her aunt replied on her behalf.

15

The parlour was only a few blocks away and she ran ahead enjoying the fresh air after the somewhat stuffy kitchen. Her new shoes didn't run that easily, but she felt like a dancer while wearing them. She held her bag and hat tight, afraid that she might lose them. The parlour was busy and she could not see the different kinds of milky delights until it was their turn. Her aunt ordered her favourites, chocolate, vanilla and strawberry. Normally she wouldn't get three scoops, but Aunt Sylvie said it was a day for a little extra.

After the ice cream, they walked to the playground, but she only played at the swings. The slide might make her dress dirty and Mama would be really upset. On a usual day, she would have wanted to stay longer, but now she just wanted to go back home. She asked Aunt Sylvie, who looked at her watch and sighed, "Yes, I think we can go back now."

She entered the kitchen. Her mother was at the same position at the table. "Mama, where's Papa?" Aunt Sylvie spoke before her mother did. "Your dad will stay with your uncle and me for a while until he finds a new home. Don't worry though, you will see him soon." She dropped her hat and bag. Her mom started to cry."

There's a picture of me, also in black and white, that I found again when I was moving into my new home. I'm about four years old, holding the hand of a friend. One sock is up, the other down, my braids are lit up by the sunlight from behind and my bangs all over the place. I'm wearing an overcoat down to my knees and look quite happily into the camera. That little girl told stories, made up stories, and would share them with anyone that would listen.

I hope there are many more to come.

In the course of her work on human rights issues, Marije Nederveen, from the Netherlands, has travelled extensively in Asia and Africa. Marije is currently interning at the Olive Leaf Foundation, a South African based sustainable development organisation. She enjoys meeting and working with people who dedicate their time to mobilizing, motivating and empowering others, and captures her stories in blogs and pictures.

On the Road to Oman

By Sarah de Freitas

Timing is everything. In love. In friendship. At its best, good timing creates chance encounters that lead to wonderful relationships and other magical twists of fate.

In the randomness of events, two persons' paths inexplicably cross. At times, the paths converge and a bond is formed. Some time on, those same paths may separate, leaving nothing behind except memories to be relished upon as the years pass. But just because separations can be painful does not mean that we should shy away from allowing a union to be formed in the first place. Similarly, just because loving and/or being loved can be empowering does not mean that we should cling on and never let go. Indeed, it is the complexity of human interactions that brings out the richest characteristics innate to our beings.

As the wise might say, let things be.   Let life flow. Experience the moment as it is. And let the memories, wonderful or sad, good or bad, coalesce to become a part of who you are. Have no regrets. - *Ed*

~ 2 ~

It was yet another road trip with my good friend...a good friend who always pops up at the 'introns' or spaghetti-tangled moments in my life, such as when I went searching for my dad at age 19. Looking back, my friend was or is 'always there', only missing are the moments that have been edited out as unimportant on the cutting room floor of my memory.

18

I like my friend so much that even the thought of him makes me smile. Years ago he told me he was learning to fly. I hate flying and during turbulence would imagine that he was steering the plane, sitting in the cockpit with a big grin on his face. Even after he told me he'd given up flying because he wasn't any good at it, I still used his image to derive comfort...like a metaphor for safety.

I was on the road trip escaping some of my own turbulence after a three year relationship had crashed out unexpectedly. The unexpected bit included a curt e-mail and the man in question running off to the ends of the earth (on a trip to the Amazon), with his mother as a replacement companion (hmmm).

Looking back without a fog of sadness and dashed expectations etc...I was worn down in part because life had not been easy for a while. A year of feeling the relationship slip away despite my efforts had taken its toll. As a believer in working harder (works in my work life) I had 'failed'. Wise clichés such as 'it just wasn't to be', 'when one door closes another opens' are difficult to swallow when in free fall.

A 'broken heart' is an extraordinary thing and I was baffled by how destroyed I felt...How could this be worse than the loss of a loved relative? Fortunately I had switched from a high pressure medical job to a less demanding research job and, for a time, could be dispassionate at work without it being detrimental or even noticeable. 'Time out' for emotional flailing-about prevented a stain of bitterness and lost optimism taking hold. "Give sorrow words. The grief that does not speak whispers the o'er-fraught heart, and bids it break." - *Shakespeare.*

...So, in a jeep heading from Dubai to Oman with my friend, I was very much at the emotional flailing-about stage and giving sorrow far, far too many very repetitive words...and my poor friend listened to this and that about my ex for seven days. He is a far better listener than I am and he is also someone whose opinion is always utterly unexpected and yet instantly believable. It's as if he sees the missing part of my perception and he does not allow me an easy ride in conversation either. He challenges me and told me many times as we bumped along that dusty road what a great guy my ex sounded like from what I was saying, which I found really irritating though obviously I'd liked my ex for a reason!

To be fair, my ex had never done anything bad apart from allowing me to think that we were forever for a while after he'd stopped feeling it, thus wasting my time (fertility) but not his own... My female friends were compassionate but much of that compassion followed a "men are mean" format... Which had its place (anger) in the grief cycle but at some point I needed to leave that loop, recalibrate and tune it all out.

I still had one foot in the men-are-mean camp on this trip, which my friend approached with amusement and put his own spin on. Let me give you an example of one of our many "woman think men are mean but men might be thinking women can be even meaner" conversations...In this instance we were talking about why some husbands cheat on their wives soon after the birth of a first child.

Me: *It's terrible... and just because that woman is not so sexy and starts pampering the baby instead of her brat of a husband he runs off with someone who's got time to dress up and flatters his ego more.*

Friend: *...But hang on a minute what if that woman never really loved the guy and just married him for the money, baby and security (chequebook with sperm scenario). What if once the baby's born she turns mean and lets herself go as she's already got all that she ever wanted from the relationship and he realizes the whole thing was a sham...*

Makes you think, I suppose.

My friend and I drove around for about a week. The stars by the sea at night in Oman are bright enough to lift the heaviest of hearts. It was deeply nourishing to break from normal worldly ties to talk about sadness, but also about life.

We went back to Dubai for a couple of days, and on the day of my flight to London he announced feelings for me. Given my droning on about my ex during the week, it took me by surprise. I had been too deep in my own preoccupation to observe my attentive listener. I had not even reached the 'first cut is the deepest' stage (Cat Stevens) when one can just about give scraps of one's heart to someone new. Despite a wrong turn in the road to the airport I made the flight. I'm sorry to say it but I really needed to make that flight. I could not give what was deserved.

I thought intensely on the plane, looking back at everything we'd talked about. It sounded different knowing how it must have made the listener feel and also trying to figure out what the future now held. I landed feeling more optimistic and it was not long before I was on a plane again to see him, perhaps still a bit before the bandages should have come off. We did not work out. Not in a bad way. The strength of the friendship barely flickered and we are always able to be happy for each other.

Thinking about my friend still makes me smile but I'm in love with somebody new and so is he.

Sarah de Freitas' heritage is Portuguese, but she was born and raised in England. She is a doctor, and lives in London.

I'm Fat

By Chè Monique Young

> Some time ago, I asked the husband-to-be of a good friend, "What do you love about her?" He replied unequivocally, "Her confidence". This was my first revelation that self-assuredness in a woman could be beautiful and a powerful source of attraction.
>
> How often do we allow advertisements to bombard us with lofty promises of beauty enhancing treatments? How many hours do we spend in front of the mirror wistfully thinking of all the changes we want to make to our bodies?
>
> Chè's story flies in the face of these 'image destroyers' and 'soul depleters'. It is a tale of coming of age — the winding road of becoming comfortable with who we are, and learning to love ourselves. We are reminded that, in whatever shape or form, we are part of nature. There is beauty in nature. And there is beauty in being natural. - *Ed*

~ 3 ~

I'm fat. I have been as long as I can remember. I'm not sure how I feel about that. Fat is a very loaded word and fat is what I am. Fat is not like ugly. Fat is not an annoying voice. Fat isn't ditzy or being a bitch. Those things, while people may not like them, are accepted as permanent characteristics of a person. Being fat, however, comes with the expectation that you are unhappy and trying hard to get rid of it. But I'm tired of being unhappy with half of my physical self and wishing it away.

Perhaps to make sense of how this all began, I treat the story of my fat like it's folklore or a fairy tale.

Once upon a time there was a beautiful girl named Donna. She was tall, skinny and athletic. She went to a private school and preferred to wear boys' blazers because her limbs were so long. She finished high school when afros were fashionable and a huge round 'fro haloed her head in her senior year photo. Donna went off to college and met a dangerous and exciting man named Tim. Donna and Tim wed in 1980. They had a spectacular ceremony – people still talk about it thirty years later.

Five years after they married, Donna became pregnant. Everyone was excited. This baby was to be the first grandchild on both sides of the family. In fact, so many people were eagerly anticipating the new arrival that Donna was given at least four baby showers.

At last the baby was born, Chè Robyn-Monique Young. Chè was a small baby even by '80s standards, weighing in at six pounds, ten ounces. She could not fit into the homecoming outfit that Donna had carefully picked out. Stockings hung off her legs making her look like a tiny bird.

Donna was so concerned about how little her baby was that she weighed Chè daily on a kitchen scale. She also prayed that the baby would become plump. Miracle of miracles, Chè packed on the pounds. In fact, by the time she was a toddler, her father had taken to calling her 'bruiser'.

Poor Donna was still not happy. While she wanted a chubby baby, she did not want a fat child, especially not a fat daughter. There was nothing Donna could do; she had prayed for her baby to gain weight and that's precisely what happened. Donna tried everything to undo her prayer so that this girl, by now no-longer-so little, could be as beautiful and skinny as her mother. While Chè was in elementary school, Donna put her on numerous diets including the 'Cabbage Soup diet' and 'Fit For Life'. Donna would send Chè to school

23

with lunch boxes packed with breadless sandwiches: lettuce wrapped around lunch meat, and a pickle. On occasion, lunch would consist entirely of a quarter of a watermelon. The kids at school found Chè's lunches to be quite peculiar. When other kids were busy with extracurricular activities, Chè was at home following the routine of an aerobics video. Over time, Donna partook in these slimming plans as well. Donna was never 'fat', but she was not happy with the way her body was changing; a once tiny waist-line was starting to succumb to several pregnancies and, frankly, to life itself. She was now trying to drop between five and thirty pounds at any given point. When Donna was pregnant with her third child, nine year old Chè weighed more than she did. After Donna gave birth, she and Chè joined Weight Watchers.

As Chè got older, Donna resorted to bribery, promising her beautiful leather and fur coats if she could just drop the pounds. But that didn't work. She then told Chè that boys and, later, men would be more interested in her if she were thin. But Chè never slimmed. Her weight would always be the elephant in the room for those two. They couldn't break bread, go shopping or plan an activity without the weight issue coming up.

I wish I could tell the story of my fat, of my weight, of my insecurities without discussing my mother. She isn't fat. She isn't me. It is true that, somehow very early in my life, possibly from the very day I was born when she decided I was too small and something had to be done about that, my mother had rooted herself deeply into the aspect of creating the perfect physique for me. Yet, there's more to my fat than my mother and that's what I would like to talk about.

I've always been a little odd. Smart, assertive, and independent, I never quite fit in anywhere, not at any time in my life. I generally attributed this to being fat, rather than my, shall we call it, 'quirky personality'. I was slower in speed than other kids, bad at sports and boys didn't like me.

Not being a fashionista herself, as a child my mother dressed me in men's pants that were too small and oversized men's t-shirts. Through elementary and middle school I would have to lie flat on my back to squeeze into a pair of jeans, and then sit uncomfortably through class all day with my legs sandwiched like a couple of sardines in that 'one-size-too-small' outfit. If ever there were a special event and I needed to dress up for it, invariably I'd end up resembling a grandma.

By middle school, I'd accepted that boys would never like me. I was fat, black and ugly. I was the fat friend. In fact, throughout middle school, high school and college, if I were attending a co-ed event, I understood clearly that the boys would be interested in all my friends, but never in me.

In gym class in the 7th grade, Steven teased me for having hairy legs so I decided to exclusively wear trousers. Later that summer, Alex, an older boy on whom I had a major crush, joked about the fat lumps on my upper arms that looked like muscles. From then on I never wore tank tops. I endured one or two very hot summers of long jeans and big shirts before I had my first epiphany. You can't hide fat. It wouldn't matter if I wore a burqa or a bikini, I would still look fat.

Naked Chè was born. I started wearing clothes that were less oppressive. I found that the fewer clothes I wore, the more comfortable I was. I was making quite a bit of money babysitting at this point and spent the overwhelming majority of it on clothing and Frappacinos. From ages 14 to 23, I dressed like a bit of a skank. I wasn't fond of wearing bras despite having size 40DD breasts. Because they weren't comfortable. Comfort and cuteness were now the driving factors in my choice of attire. Because I was always flitting about in a state of partial nudeness, people simply assumed that I was really comfortable in my own skin. The truth is, like everyone else, sometimes I was, and sometimes I just wasn't.

What really helped me to become comfortable in my own skin was the mirror. Through high school I, like many adolescents, would spend hours staring at myself. I was constantly evaluating and reevaluating myself. In the process I became desensitized to my size and began to see beyond it.

The more I looked at 'the fat', the less it disgusted me. The more innocuous it became. I realized it wasn't ugly.

I also began to take note of the fact that fat feels good. It is soft and warm. The kids I babysat loved for me to hold and hug them. I guess that meant that fat could be comforting.

Through looking at myself, touching myself and realizing that self hatred is not productive, I began to love who I am.

This was not a magical development. Nobody sneakily sprinkled fairy dust while I slept allowing me to somehow awake as the spokeswoman for happy, fat girls. Instead, it was a process of sorts. Over time, I began to develop certain core beliefs about myself and the world. One is that it's OK to be fat and if someone has a problem with fat, that's their problem not mine. Another is that I'm incredibly sexy. Sexy, I've learned over the years, is quite a super power.

When I was about 16 or 17, I read about Big Burlesque in San Francisco – an entire troupe of fat ladies who were sexy as hell and embraced it. These women strutted their stuff half-naked but in surprisingly tasteful outfits, like Parisien damsels in feathers and ruffles at the Moulin Rouge in days gone by. They used their body not just to entertain men, but to tell a story for which the opening line was *"You come here to look at me because I am the essence of woman; because I am beautiful."*

I dreamed of running away and joining them, but when I was 21, I realized I didn't have to go very far. I discovered the DC Gurly Show, a local burlesque troupe made up of women of all body types, age, sexual orientation and gender identity. I decided that I liked this inclusivity even more than I liked the idea of Big Burlesque. Where Big Burlesque says that fat women are sexy, the DC Gurly Show says that **all** people are sexy. There's no othering or qualifying involved.

I joined the troupe in 2007 and loved having an outlet to be openly sexual and overtly sensual without anyone expecting me to first apologize for being fat.

Right now, I am one of the more confident people I know. I want to just say *"I'm fat, so what"*? And, in many ways, that's what I do. I don't let being fat hold me back or stop me from living life to the fullest. But fat, like I said earlier, is still complicated.

While I can accept my fat from a beauty and self esteem perspective, a lot of the world doesn't. Being fat limits my dating options, clothing options, job options. It affects my fertility and chances of having a healthy pregnancy, chances of living a long life and increases my risks of developing heart disease, diabetes, cancer and other major illnesses. So, to say that it's OK to be fat or that I'm not going to make any effort to lose weight seems like I'm giving up on myself.

How can I intelligently accept that?

I've been on and off diets my whole life and I'm tired of it. I can't look you in the eye and promise to start eating healthier and exercising for 'my wellbeing'. See, when I do those things, I'm not thinking about lower blood pressure or higher energy levels. I'm really thinking about smaller pants sizes and more men finding me attractive.

In fact, I'm currently trying to convince myself to lose 80 pounds by Halloween so I can dress up as Beyoncé.

But, hopefully as I continue to mature I'll find a contented place and make decisions driven more by what makes me healthy. Who knows what the future holds. Right now I'm fat. I'm confident. I'm sexy. I'm conflicted. I'm imperfect. I'm at risk for all sorts of problems. I'm happy. I'm human.

Chè Monique Young was raised in and currently resides in Alexandria, Virginia (US). She holds a Bachelor's Degree in Women's Studies from Temple University and is a massage therapist, belly dancer and burlesque performer. Chè is currently planning workshops to help women tap in to their own 'sexy' and let go of unnecessary baggage related to body image.

The Tea Lady in the Boardroom

By Zipho Sikhakhane

It is not often that one is so inspired by a young colleague. When it does happen, one pauses to reflect upon the beauty of life, then doubles up on pace to make up for time lost in experiencing its richness.

Zipho's life reads like an opera - growing up in the new nation of South Africa, in an environment of poverty and sicknesses and a world where both her skin colour and gender have been and, in some instances, still are discriminated against. Despite her youth, she has faced many challenges, many of which both pain and inspire at once. Zipho has triumphed above them beyond belief. She reminds me of fresh buds in spring, bursting with hope, resilience and energy after a savage winter. She is the future that the end of apartheid had hoped for and a fountain of strength from which we can all draw. - *Ed*

~ 4 ~

Here I am sitting at a long oval table, which looks exactly like the ones I have seen on television. Black leather seats, flowers and paintings all around the room. I am clicking away at the back of my pen, wearing a black fancy suit like everyone else. There is a side table with teacups, saucers and spoons placed neatly next to a pile of biscuits. I have imagined this day for many years now, the very moment where I finally feel like *I have made it*! Today marks my first boardroom meeting.

When the meeting commences, my mother walks in wearing a black and white apron and she starts serving the tea around the table. It is customary in African culture that I see every Black Woman as my Mother and every Black Man as my Father. By instinct I want to get up and help her serve the tea to everyone. After all, I was raised to be a good servant. My brain quickly reminds that I should not do that in a board meeting. Rather, I should continue with the discussions at hand and ignore what is happening in the background. I pretend to concentrate, although the urge to assist constantly nags at me, as my mother serves one cup after another. My turn for tea arrives and all I do is smile and say thank you.

The sound of the shutting door upon her exit brings sadness to my eyes since I have just betrayed my own cultural norms. A glance across the room makes me realise that no one else here can relate to this– I am the only black woman present! Everyone else is white, male and decades older than I am. In contrast, they look comfortable, so much at ease, as if they have done this for centuries! Big English words dropped from one mouth to another, as page by page the discussion document is being presented. I turn into a mute and begin praying for the earth to swallow me up, especially now as the others have started sneaking glimpses in my direction! Perhaps I am not the only one feeling uneasy with my presence.

The big question of how I landed myself in this exclusive boardroom starts to linger in my head. My brain reminds me: it is just the outcome of a little girl's dream to make it big in business against all the odds! This is the very room I have spent all my life hoping to get into. Even today, in the New South Africa, when a girl child is raised well in the poor black community, her future is defined as a wife, a house cleaner or a tea lady. The ambitious ones become teachers or nurses. None of these really appealed to me because I was the 'societal non-conformer' – a term I invented to describe an innate need not to let my future be defined by the views of other human beings. I inevitably aimed for the businesswoman route because this would get me a ticket into the exclusive boardroom I had dreamt about. I ignored the words of discouragement and numerous giggles received when I shared this dreamed-up tale with others. I wanted to beat the odds and this meant I needed to deviate from seeing the future in South Africa as a divided field comprised of black careers and white careers.

I see myself as the empty vessel that makes the loudest noise. Unlike the vessel though, when it came to the crunch, I would make sure my vessel was full and showed no signs of inadequacy. Starting with my grades in school, I tried to push them to perfection. This involved ensuring that there were matches and candles on standby, given that power outages were quite common when I tried to study late into the night. I kept this up all the way through to university and even resorted to sitting in cold rooms in the middle of the night just so I could fight the urge to fall asleep. Eventually my academic record was good enough for me to walk the talk, but somehow I needed to learn how to talk the talk in the proper way.

Her name was Brooke Logan, a beautiful blonde character in the American soap opera *The Bold and the Beautiful*. Lines uttered with elegance, her vocabulary always contained some strange English word that I had never heard before. The perfect role model to mimic. Every day at 6pm I would get my dictionary, turn on the television and glue myself to the screen for the next half hour. The dictionary eventually fell to bits because I had flicked through it in many rushed moments to interpret every new word Brooke had uttered. Occasionally, I would go into momentary distress when words such as "bouquet" or "rendezvous" were used, since their pronunciations are nothing close to how they are written in the dictionary!

Eventually I could walk and talk right, but somehow I needed *evidence* of my worthiness to be in that dimly lit meeting room that would define my success.

In between my school lectures, I completed every part time job that would have me. That way I would have a stream of people ready to vouch for my proficiency should the need arise. I knew I had somewhat surpassed this goal when one interviewer looked at me in shock and said, "So you are *Superwoman*?" She was serious and not the first to use this term. I had been a receptionist, tutor, shop keeper, entertainer, speaker, writer, auditor, all in one year – you name it, I have done it.

I eventually believed I was ready to try out the boardroom and chose a career that granted an entry ticket for the young professional. Management consulting presented me with the key to enter. The only trick was that I had to work hard so that my manager would reward me with the privilege of joining the client's management team in the boardroom. That moment had finally arrived.

South Africa is no longer a divided country – my attendance in this meeting is evidence that it is possible for minorities to cross the line. My heart is supposed to be doing a little dance in celebration given this is what I have long coveted. Instead I feel like an alien – not the one with three eyes, but rather a different sex altogether – with thick lips, coarse hair and a somewhat burned complexion. An alien who deserted her roots by not getting on her knees and serving everyone tea in the respectable fashion that her own mother had taught her. My culture commands that I never sit on the chair if any man is around – it is a sign of disrespect. Yet here I am sitting at the same table with males and no one thought to bring a floor mat for me to sit on in the corner. Business etiquette commands that I look people in the eye when I speak to them, else I will be mistrusted or, construed to have low self-confidence. My culture scorns any woman who looks an elderly person in the eye, especially when addressing them. The rules are simple: lower your head, join your hands together, and speak quietly – not in this loud commanding voice that I am expected to project in the room, certainly not with my hands above the table, and perhaps even waving them around while I speak to assert a point. I should be giving precedence to the opinions of my superiors, not challenging discussion points that I disagree with.

While everyone else was busy tackling the business problem at hand, I was distracted with my own internal battles – fighting to prevent my culture from creeping into the boardroom setting, for fear that I may never ever be invited to attend these meetings again. At the same time I caution my instincts not to erase the behaviours which my family and community have taught me – especially since I needed to exercise these when I get home. I am reminded that at home the business suit comes off and the pants will be replaced with a long, respectable skirt. I will be acting in the traditions of any well-raised Zulu woman. I will receive my orders for the day and respectively oblige without showing any signs of restraint.

It would be a waste if I choose to discard my culture and its teachings from here onwards; after all who ever said being different was something to be ashamed of? Perhaps embracing some elements of my culture may just help me last longer than the typical person in this boardroom world.

For one, meetings always reach a juncture where people start being harsh as they linger and argue about one discussion point. I know I will never be caught in the heat of these arguments as being humble and maintaining composure is part of my cultural blueprint. I am scarcely given occasion to express an opinion in my culture, so whenever I get the chance I use it right. The fact that at home I am on my knees, in respect to whoever is in the room, means I am not afraid to push aside my perspective and consider the views of others. Because my eye is no regular playing field, my big idea or final price can never be predicted by my business associates until I verbalise it. That big idea presented by an elegant black woman can never really be forgotten – my soft tone and select vocabulary means that no one else can sell it like I can. I am not one of the guys in the room.

I will not squirm when times get tough; after all, I have seen many a chicken, sheep and cow slain in front of my naked eyes, and had barely flinched at the sight. My grandmother taught me that a woman should never shy away from doing chores all day and every day – so the day will likely never come when I am worn out from yet another late night at the office. When the business makes a profit, it is not my own needs and wants that I think of. Instead, I imagine how I can invest it back into the community. After all, I am already used to spreading my pay check among at least fifteen relatives.

Everyone gets up and starts shaking hands and exchanging business cards – the meeting is over. My manager whispers in my ear that I need to quickly follow through on some queries that had arisen during the discussion. I nod, even though I had heard none of these queries. My thoughts had been lost in the puzzle of a divided life. The tea lady walks back in to collect the cups and realises that I had stayed behind to help pack everything away. She flashes a smile of pride that could only mean one thing, "I wish she were my daughter."

We eventually leave the boardroom together and, frankly, I still do not know which role I was destined to play in that room: the tea lady or the businesswoman.

Dadewethu Ntombazane Mfazi Nkosikazi, Lalela!

[English: My lady, woman, wife, Listen!]

She screams of pain

Everyone smiles

And no one sees her pain

Let's rejoice, the baby is born!

The bitch of the town, she is called

Family wrecker, her middle name
The married lover was drawn to her charm
'tis not his fault
The woman takes all the blame.

Scars and memory she must bear
Yes, the perpetrator must be punished
Let's discuss HIS sentence!
What of the pain of the rape victim
      The punching bag
      The kitchen slave
      The toilet cleaner
Oh gosh, what of the mere rib of Adam?

Who are we? "Women"???
Is there more to us than just
Breasts, looks, hair, curves and make up?
Do we exist just to WOO men.
Or are we women because we are
      Mothers of the nations
      Sisters of the universe
      Daughters of fallen leaders
Or maybe, just maybe
We are the...
...shush, listen, hear for I will explain.

Women are
Symbols of happiness
New life just when humanity thought all was over

Oh yes, we breed sunshine on those cold days

That string of masculinity, just when all men gave up.

We are like those mere seeds

That emerge into trees

And bring out beautiful fruits!

Quite vulnerable on the outside

Yes we admit

But strong, firm, mighty on the inside!

How else could we have mothered all the leaders of this world?

How else could we still stand and celebrate after so many struggles?!

'Pass laws' we protested

And many more we shall change

Ah yes, we can make much change

Because, when placed together

We are like dynamite!!!

The roads are still far

The gaps in the system still exist

But we will strive

Ah yes we will

For we are the rainbow to this world of thunderstorms.

Uma uke wathinta umfazi

Wathi ukum' nyakazisa nje

Uzobe uthinte imbokodo!

[English: If you ever touch a woman

Even a slight nudge,

You have struck a rock!]

Zipho Sikhakhane was born and raised in the new South Africa. She dreams big dreams and yet remains grounded in how she relates to friends and family. Zipho has a passion for transforming organisations in Africa using the qualities that make her different. She grew up hand to mouth and had to persevere to make it through the system by starting up multiple small business ventures to support her living expenses. She hopes to inspire other young women to beat the odds in their lives, believing that anything is possible and striving to make this an everyday reality.

Transitions

By Aida Axelsson-Bakri

I remember sitting next to Aida in grade 3 at the International School of Lusaka, wondering how this peculiar girl, who was the second youngest student in class and, frankly speaking, a bit of a nerd, was so incredibly popular with everyone? Rather than be jealous, Kirstin, a Scottish-Italian classmate, was her BFF (best friend forever). As was Fiona from Mauritius. Aida's grades were good. Her skinny legs navigated the cross-country track effortlessly. Her mixed-kid hair was dark golden and tangle-free. Needless to say, Aida was also our teacher's pet! How was this possible? Perhaps it's genetically ingrained? Maybe preordained from some good deed in a previous life? Who knows!

The fact is that, despite leading what many would consider a charmed life, Aida has had her share of hurdles, and has had to put some real effort into fitting in. But each little challenge has been an opportunity to step up her game, work that bit harder, and be that much more creative. The result is proof that, with a bit of luck, being a bit different can be a lot of fun! - *Ed*

~ 5 ~

I could hardly believe my luck. I and my sixth grade classmates in Lusaka, that is. *We* could hardly believe our luck. It was just odd. Why on Earth would they do that? And why weren't our parents as excited as we were?

It all had to do with 'transition'.

I always wondered what that meant, actually. Why didn't they just call it what it was: 7th grade. No. At the International School of Lusaka, they happened to call it *Transition*. And on that particularly happy day... they cancelled it! So, in effect, three classes of 6th graders – 90 odd students – were informed that they would not be coming back in the new school year to "Transition", instead they would all be coming back in the new school year to "Form One", which was, in fact, 8th grade.

Never mind why they cancelled it, or how the teachers hoped to deal with the academic material we would be missing out on. This class was delighted that we would be skipping one entire year of school!

And I was especially thrilled.

Reason being that I was always one to try to speed things up, go a bit quicker, learn a bit faster, become autonomous, and be my own boss (figuratively speaking, that is). And to cut a long story short, I somehow managed to graduate from high school and start university in Brussels at the age of 16.

So my story starts here. And for somebody who puts a lot of emphasis on anniversaries, I astoundingly realized that I missed my 20-years-in-Belgium anniversary by a few days. Yet, I am prepared to celebrate this with fireworks if anyone at all would find that a good enough reason to party with me.

It's been a good two decades in this small country and I'd like to take you down memory lane, with all the trials along the way, and a few select 'gems' within each of these transitions.

Chapter 1: 1990, and too young for a bank account

By all standards, I was a tad young to be starting university, living independently, and we all knew it: both my parents - who were always very generous with my freedom whilst keeping a protective watch at all times - and I. And I would even go so far as to say I was embarrassed of my age to the point that I would avoid any questions related to it like the plague.

Luckily for me, most people simply assumed I was average freshman age, and never bothered to ask. And had it not been for some overly helpful professors who shouted out loud, "Oh! *You're* the 16-year-old!" for all to hear, I might actually have gotten away incognito.

I distinctly remember my 17th birthday. Some friends had crafted a beautiful, almost life size, birthday card with a caricature of me on it! And it read: "*17 and finally a lady!*" It was so true. I couldn't believe how they'd hit the nail on the head. It was as though I needed to get over that threshold in order to be accepted as a person, let alone a lady, and do away with having been fast-tracked through school just by chance.

But the bank still wouldn't let me open an account on my own, or perform any operations, really. I was allowed to withdraw money but only at the counter, certainly not from an ATM, and could only make transfers with the prior approval from my parents. This was how it was – until I was 18.

It wasn't only the bank that gave me trouble. Getting a phone or cable TV (not that I could afford it anyway) was the same. Prior approval from Dad came first. Come to think of it, I couldn't even get an ID card without someone's signature.

Chapter 2: 1992, Too foreign to live here

Initially, when I moved to Belgium, I was meant to stay with a host family. It was only logical. So after registering at the university, my mother and I went to the administration office dealing with the host family kids and we queued forever.

By the time we finally got to the front of the line, I had already made my first friends. In fact, the girl in front of me who apparently 'took my host family' (some administrative hiccup) ended up being my flatmate later (after her host family's dog ate her homework a few too many times) and she is one of my best friends till now.

To make a long story short, the host family option fell through and I had to find a place to live on my own.

For the first studio apartment I lived in, I got lucky. No trouble at all. However, the hunt for a place big enough to share with a flatmate proved to be something else. "Vous avez quelle nationalité?" we would be asked via the parlophone at the door of some of the prospective apartments. "Suisse et allemande" we would say, which was true enough – to the extent that we were both half these nationalities (the other half being slightly more exotic). The problem was that neither of us resembled the (half) blue-eyed Swiss or German girls that some of the landlords were expecting. This seemed to be such an issue that on a few occasions we literally had the door slammed in our faces.

Just to give us the flavour of true xenophobia that was (and still is) alive and well in some parts of Europe, our experiences ranged from being 'randomly' picked out to be searched for drugs by cops in Gare du Midi after coming off a late night train, to being denied entry into discothèques. Oh, my circle of very international friends and I had our share of discrimination and I'm afraid it had a lot less to do with our (not so) dodgy characters than our true colours.

But we were young, and managed to get through the transition. We learned to brush it off and not waste time trying to prove ill-doers wrong, as these were isolated cases in an otherwise rather tolerant society. Still, we learned with the rise of the right wing political parties in some Belgian cities to be careful not to ruffle too many feathers as our safety could be at stake. And we repeated the mantra: rise above it.

Chapter 3: 1996, Too qualified for a job

Quality of life got better in Belgium when I stopped having to depend on public transportation to get around. I noticed a distinct improvement in my wellbeing not only because I was walking and cycling and getting a lot of fresh air, but also because I didn't have to wait at wet and windy bus stops for buses that would all be going the opposite direction and then raise my blood pressure by dashing madly for a tram and metro to get to the university's medical campus where all the life science courses were taught.

And then I embarked on the unforgiving task of trying to find a job, smack in the middle of the 1995 recession. Months went by with hardly any job ads appearing in the papers and, when they did, the competition for these positions was ferocious. For jobs in Brussels, even junior positions, one had to have 1-2 years' experience, a master's degree and four or more languages. Needless to say it was a daunting process.

I busied myself at the language school where I had been working part-time on and off during my university years, until the day a dear Norwegian friend from university called to ask whether I could step in for her as a receptionist at EFTA just for one month in the summer. She had planned to work there herself, but had a change of plan and suddenly thought I might be interested. As a Swiss citizen, I was actually the right nationality for a change!

I applied, interviewed and got the job to start immediately, on a limited duration contract of one month. First I had to learn to operate the switchboard. That was fine. Then I had to learn the names of the people who worked a few floors higher up in the building. That was not fine. Not fine at all.

EFTA is the secretariat of the European Free Trade Association, made up of four European nations: Iceland, Norway, Switzerland and Liechtenstein. And almost all members of staff originate from these four countries. It was my first contact with Icelandic names, and I had no idea how to pronounce them. In addition to that, the two drivers (a very funny Belgian duo) who hung around the reception for most of the time when they were not out driving the directors, were of absolutely no help whatsoever.

Half way into my first day, I realized I would not last long in the reception if I didn't figure out a way to learn these names fast! How to get the right intonation? How to figure out if they were male or female! I somehow managed to solve one part of these mysterious appellations: if a surname ended in "---dottir", then they would be, without a doubt, female. If it ended in"—son" that would be a male. However, this only solved part of the problem, and so I would stay up late several nights in a row memorizing the pronunciations of the names of my new colleagues! I am fairly certain that this extra effort, silly as it sounds to me now, was key to getting 'very good receptionist' status within a very short time!

They asked me to stay another month. And I did. I loved my job. Then they asked me whether I could cover for one of the secretaries that was going on maternity leave for a few months. I did. They asked me if I would cover for another secretary, and another, until I had finally worked in all the different units of the organization and got myself a splendid overview of how EFTA worked and the overall European political environment.

And after a year there, one of the heads of unit sat me down and said: "Aida, don't get stuck here; You should move on and find yourself a job related to what you have studied." The news dropped like a lead balloon. I was perfectly happy with the job(s) they had provided me, and the only drawback I could see was that these were temporary positions. But he was right, and for the first time I began to realise that I had the potential to choose what I wanted to do. So I undertook to get a career going on the basis of the unimaginable and unexpected boost this job had given to my self-confidence.

So, Brussels or elsewhere - Europe, Africa, US, I tried to find a job knowing full well that I wouldn't want to stray too far from my soul-mate and boyfriend-now-husband.

With a little bit of guidance from colleagues at work, and a very kind attaché at the Swiss Mission to the EU, I was accepted for a traineeship at the European Commission in the Directorate dealing with Research, and more specifically in the unit dealing with Biotechnology. That seemed serious enough.

Chapter 4: 1997-2001, Too happy to change

My traineeship didn't last long, just a short 5 months. But it was the perfect bridge between EFTA and the consulting jobs that came after it. As a matter of fact, with hindsight, I don't think I could have qualified for my first consulting job had I not had the experience I had in the Commission.

And that whole story is a strange one, too. On the day after the end of my traineeship, I decided to have lunch with one of my closest friends from work (the only remaining Irish member of the staff). I had planned to do a tour of the recruitment agencies in the area and used the opportunity to say hello to her. The intense search for a job was producing no results and, the best I could hope for was to get a letter saying "We will keep your CV on file for future reference". So recruiting agencies were my only hope and even then I tended to gravitate towards the administrative positions knowing that, despite holding a degree, I felt comfortable organising and assisting more qualified people than myself!

It was on the way out of the office that I ran into one of my favourite former bosses in the corridor who asked me what my plans were 'for the future'. I said that the Commission traineeship was over and that I was now officially on the job market again. He explained that he was clearing out his office and leaving EFTA to join an EU transport policy consultancy the following week. All that sounded fine and I wished him well in his new endeavours, not realising that our futures would be inter-linked for many more years to come.

As chance would have it, I received a phone call from him that very afternoon during which he told me that the firm he was joining was looking to recruit a junior consultant. And for a full 2 hours thereafter he proceeded to tell me why *I* would be perfect for the post. So I applied, interviewed, and within a few days, got myself a new, more real than real, job – all thanks to him and the incredible coincidence of crossing paths.

It was a fantastic environment. Small company. Highly specialized and experienced bosses, and I learned a lot.

I spent three and a half years in that environment and was saddened when the company suffered an unfortunate sequence of events which led to him, me and one other colleague to depart and set up our own little business.

Starting a company in a very heavily-burdened-by-red-tape country like Belgium was no easy task. In fact, I would venture to say that I had to re-encounter a number of earlier life trials to varying degrees during that process. My age (still too young to be taken seriously – at least back then!), my nationality (not being from an EU country in particular), my qualifications (or lack of), all came up at one point or another, again and again, as challenges. Not to mention that I had no particular business skills or training. I learned to think logically, practically, and not put too much emphasis on *how things should be* but rather on *how things are* and how I *would want things to be*. And together, we managed to create a very pleasant and self-empowering business environment.

Chapter 5: 2011, Too good to be true

Today, I'm truly blessed to be living happily in Belgium with my husband and two children. I now run the same company on my own and, together with my colleagues, provide strategic advice on EU policy. We work on interesting topics that motivate us, and refuse to work on matters that we consider unethical or where we have conflicts of personal or business interest.

I struggle with the work-life balance, especially in the mornings when I'm trying to get out of the house with the kids, or in the evenings when I'm trying to get dinner on the table... But those are classics!

In truth, I'm grateful every day that a particular individual came along at each of my transitions. They have believed in me and given me a chance at the unlikeliest of times. Call it serendipity; call it luck. But with all the benefits of hindsight, it has simply been too good to be true.

Aida Axelsson-Bakri was born in Ethiopia to a Swiss mother and an Ethiopian father. She grew up in Uganda, Kenya, Zambia, and Nigeria, where her father worked with the UN, before moving at the age of 16 to study in Brussels. She worked as an EU policy consultant for nearly 4 years before starting her own consultancy focusing on EU transport, environment, energy and health policy. Aida is married to an Ethiopian-Swede, William, with whom she went to school in Zambia from the age of 8. This truly international couple are now happily rooted in Belgium, where they are raising their two children to be citizens of the world.

Suddenly, Without A Map

By Winnie M. Li

This is the longest and one of the most emotive stories in the collection. I made a conscious decision not to edit it for length so it retains its original subtleties and depth. Reading it for the first time, I found myself led through a long and dark tunnel, and praying very hard for the glimpse of light that would mark its end.

I am grateful that wounds heal. I am even more grateful for the things on Earth that help wounds heal – family, friends, medicine, money, time. May all who are wounded find the cocoon that provides you with that precious shelter. - *Ed*

~ 6 ~

"Can you help me? I think I'm lost and don't know where I'm going."

A fifteen-year-old boy says this to me, and there is something odd and untraceable in his pale eyes as he approaches. I'm walking through Colin Glen Forest Park in West Belfast on a Saturday afternoon. As a Chinese-American, I'm an obvious foreigner in this part of town, so it's strange that he would ask *me* for directions. But I do my best to help anyway.

"Over in that direction is the Falls Road..." I start to explain.

It's a beautiful spring afternoon in 2008, and I'm in a good mood, having just begun to unwind from three busy days of meetings and conferences in Northern Ireland. Tomorrow, I'll be flying back to London to attend the red carpet premiere of a film I'd helped to produce. Today, I've set aside time to hike along an 11-mile trail described in my Lonely Planet guidebook, starting in this city park and extending up to the north of Belfast. It's a little reward for myself, a chance to bask in nature, and escape the whirl of social events and work commitments which make my life so busy.

I am twenty-nine-years-old, driven, professional, ambitious, and I have a Plan.

That Plan does not include getting randomly assaulted and raped by a fifteen-year-old stranger.

In fact, the Plan was all together different, a script for achievement and happiness. It had been instilled in me by my immigrant parents, who moved to America as graduate students from Taiwan. And it went something like this: study hard, get into a good university (Harvard, preferably), establish a prosperous career, start a family, make your parents proud.

Most of my life, I'd developed variations on the Plan. Like when I decided to study Folklore and Mythology at Harvard, instead of preparing for medical school. Or when I became addicted to traveling on my own, backpacking through Germany at the age of nineteen so I could write for a travel guidebook. Or when I moved to London at twenty-three, without a work visa, chasing down the slim possibility of working for a film producer I had met once. Most of the time I managed to get things to work, somehow balancing my over-achiever ethic with my thrill for adventure and the unknown.

But that afternoon, this fifteen-year-old boy in Belfast presented a completely different kind of unknown to me.

After all, no one ever plans to put "Rape Victim" on their CV.

None of this is on my mind as I continue hiking in the park that afternoon, the fifteen-year-old still trying to make incoherent conversation with me. In my typical driven fashion, I am eager to get on with the trail, and I don't want this kid tagging along. But every few minutes, he keeps showing up, as if he's playing some kind of game, following me deeper and deeper into the less populated parts of the park.

An uncomfortable feeling tells me there's something weird going on, but I'm not going to stop hiking just because of some annoying kid.

And when I confront him for the third and final time, by the edge of the forest, it's too late. There's nobody else around, and the nearest busy road is 500 meters away, across an empty, derelict wasteland. As he emerges from the bushes this time, an unfamiliar panic rises in my gut.

"Do you like to have sex outdoors?" he asks suddenly.

Something unnatural skips in the beat of my heart. "No," I say firmly, and I turn instantly towards the busy road.

But then, it's as if a switch has been flipped.

"Stay right there, bitch!" he screams, and now I see a feral anger burning in his pale eyes. "Don't move!"

Taken aback, I try to make frantic sense of the situation. Could I take him on in a physical showdown? If it weren't for my backpack, I'd be sprinting for the busy road already, but in my confusion, I hesitate.

Then he's grabbing me, pulling me towards the bushes, and I'm pushing to get free. *Don't lose your footing*, I warn myself. But the ground underneath is tricky – loose stones rattling over upturned earth, and it gives way below me, my hiking shoes slipping on the pebbles.

I am thrown to the mud – and the next moment, he is on top of me, his hands at my throat, his fist rising up to strike me on the head.

*****

Some thirty, forty minutes later, I am covered in mud and bruises. I haven't blacked out, the way they do in movies, to conveniently cut out the unpleasant part. I've been conscious through it all, and some engine-like survival instinct has kicked in, constantly reassessing the situation, trying to figure out the best solution, the most practical way to act. Have years of project management as a film producer, a decade of experience as a solo backpacker, taught me anything? I must improvise. There is no script to this. No carefully devised Plan. Nowhere on the map did the Lonely Planet mark out that here, at this point in the trail, I would encounter a troubled boy with psychopathic tendencies.

So thirty, forty minutes later, he has left – having made no attempt to take my wallet, my iPod, my phone, my watch. He got what he came for, and now he's gone.

Only then do I allow myself to cry, as I sit by the side of the path, that engine still churning away, trying to decide what to do next. Part of me wants to get up and continue the trail, strike out for the hills and escape – just so I can pretend it never happened. Yet somehow I know that realistically, that's not the responsible thing to do. My mind is unable at that moment to piece together the word "rape." But I know I need medical attention, and I know this boy deserves to be caught. So I make my decision.

Feebly, I make my way across the derelict wasteland towards the busy road. I call a friend. She calls the police. When the police find me twenty minutes later, there is the thick drawl of Belfast accents asking me if I'm ok, if I can show them the crime scene, if I can describe my attacker. That engine is racing now, spitting out details, functioning on overdrive to provide the police as much information as possible. But the heart of me – the real me –has gone into hiding. Completely shell-shocked. Silently grateful when my friends arrive, to hold my hand throughout the subsequent eight hours of questions and exams. But otherwise mute, stunned, trapped in a surreal daze.

That daze lasted for months, even years, after the day of the attack. It's as if a giant knife has just been ripped through my insides, gutting me clean, so that I'm a mere shell of who I once was. This proxy, shell-like version of me goes about living the ruins of my life, handling the mundane, day-to-day tasks of the crime procedural, the endless medical follow-up, maintaining any previous resemblance my life now has to the one before the attack.

The irony of it all, is that I had been invited to Belfast as some kind of honor. Years before, I'd been a George Mitchell Scholar, selected to serve an ambassadorial role as an American studying in Ireland on a prestigious fellowship. That week in 2008, I'd been flown to Belfast to attend a special symposium commemorating the tenth anniversary of the peace process in Northern Ireland. I used the opportunity to schedule a few meetings for an upcoming film project I hoped to produce there that year.

One minute, you're a busy, ambitious film producer, with a hyperactive social and work life. The next minute, you're a rape victim, covered in mud and bruises, the topic of tomorrow's lurid headline, another unnamed statistic in the crime log.

The absurdity is not lost on me, a day after the rape, as I struggle to attend that red-carpet premiere of a film I'd worked on. I've walked red carpets before, I'd been to the Oscars when one of our films was nominated. Working in the media, I am all too aware of the importance of image, of presenting yourself well, of projecting success and confidence. But when a truth this harsh is suddenly thrust upon you, can you maintain the right kind of image and remain genuine to yourself?

Less than twenty-four hours after the attack, I'm on a plane back to London. I've told my boss what has happened, but it's the first Leicester Square premiere for one of our films, and after my years of hard work, I'm not going to allow some 15-year-old jerk to prevent me from enjoying this.

Only, of course, he already has.

A friend meets me at the airport, takes me home, helps me into a diaphanous gown which a designer has lent me for the occasion. Long, white, in a classical Grecian style -- it's a pity I can't even appreciate it this evening. My multiple bruises are very visible, but I ignore them as I struggle to put my hair up. Another friend meets me in Leicester Square and takes me down the red carpet. Thankfully we're too late for any press or public to care who we are.

In the cinema, I am seated next to a film director I've worked with many times before. He asks me casually how I am, unaware of what's happened. I hesitate. I ask him if he wants to know the truth, and he answers, yeah, sure why not. I tell him.

Shocked, he doesn't know what to say, and eventually blurts out, gauchely: "What, he was just a kid and you couldn't fight him off?"

"No," I say, shaking my head. And that conversation is over.

After the screening, we make our way to the after-party in a trendy West End club. The low-level lighting helps to conceal my bruises, and I make small talk with the actors from our film, while sipping inventive cocktails and nibbling on canapés. On the outside, I probably seem fine. Inside, I'm hardly there.

The next morning, I start making phone calls to my doctor and the local rape crisis centre, asking what medical and psychological care I should be seeking. There's a glut of work emails in my inbox, and unable to cope, I write to one contact: "I am sorry but over the weekend, I was assaulted and raped. Could you please speak to one of my colleagues about this for the time being?"

Was it unprofessional to write that? Would it have been more professional to say I was "in an accident," when that is so far from the truth? I don't care. I now have greater concerns.

My sister arrives a few days later, having been granted time off from her law firm to fly eleven hours and see me. It is comforting to have her with me as we traipse from one hospital appointment to another. I have just enough energy to negotiate my new medical and legal responsibilities as a rape victim. Once home, I collapse uselessly on the couch while my sister takes care of food, errands, tidies my usually messy room.

We both agree the news of my attack should be kept from our parents. We don't talk at length about it, but somehow we both feel, deep down, that this kind of terrible, unexpected news might be too much for our parents to bear. That they're better off not knowing the truth. Better off thinking their youngest daughter, who graduated Summa Cum Laude from Harvard, who has been single and living on the other side of the world for eight years now, is still happily working towards a rewarding career.

I think for a moment about the kind of grief that would drown my parents once we tell them – my mom's sobbing, my dad's unspoken frustration. And I think it would be better off to spare them that. Their emotional anguish, thousands of miles away, would only make matters worse.

This one, I decide, I will have to handle on my own.

*****

The afternoon of the attack, the police ask me how I would describe myself physically, since they will need to release a physical description of both the victim and the suspected assailant, in a plea for witnesses. I describe myself as "a woman in her mid- to late-twenties. Chinese-American, slim, with long, black hair."

In Belfast, perhaps the notion of Chinese-American proves too slippery.

The following day, newspaper headlines shout: "Chinese tourist brutally raped" or "A Chinese student attacked and raped in Colin Glen Forest Park." Some journalists contact the Chinese Welfare Association in Belfast and ask them to comment on my attack. The press emphasizes that my assault happened four years ago to the day that a local teenage girl was raped and murdered in the very same park. A few days later, on a Belfast radio chat show discussing local crime, the mother of the murdered girl calls in to express sympathy for me. "My heart goes out to that wee Chinese girl," she sighs in her Northern Irish drawl.

Listening to this in my London flat, I laugh wryly. Somehow it's the omission of the word "American" which paints a completely different picture of how I would be perceived. When an old college friend hears this, he shakes his head and smirks: " 'wee Chinese girl'... You know, that's completely *not* you."

He's right. But then again, if you picture what the media expects a rape victim to be, that's completely not me, either.

Instinctively, I decide not to hide the truth from any of my close friends. However, this immediately forces me to choose whom I consider close enough. Each time I'm asked the simple question "What's up?," should I brave yet another uncomfortable conversation -- or put up a completely false façade? I insist on the truth, if I am going to consider any friendship genuine. I even send a mass email out to my friends, explaining what happened, to pre-empt having to tell the same story over and over.

My female friends, both in London and abroad, prove to be amazingly supportive, sympathetic, eager to cook me a meal or send me a care package. Several of them share the stories of their own rape, or of their sister, aunt, cousin who had been raped. None of these stories I'd ever heard before.

The men react less helpfully. Unsure of what to say, some take weeks to email back after I tell them what had happened. Others freeze upon hearing the truth.

It is this awkward reaction I try to avoid, but pretending to be normal in any social situation now seems tantamount to lying to myself. How can I be "normal" when I'm plagued daily by claustrophobia, nausea, unpredictable bouts of crying? I used to be able to backpack through foreign countries on my own. Now, even venturing outside my apartment causes panic. I once could befriend complete strangers on a train. But if a fifteen-year-old boy can do this to you, who *can* you trust? These days, I can't even handle meeting acquaintances. Or if I do, it involves erecting a thin, flimsy façade of "normality," which threatens to collapse at any moment.

Unfortunately, I have to attend three weddings within six months of my attack. I'm to be a bridesmaid at the wedding of an ex-flatmate in July. A few weeks earlier, her hen weekend kicks off on a Friday night at a louche, opulent nightclub in Camden called Gilgamesh. Earlier that afternoon, I'm scheduled to visit the Southwark Police Station, so I can identify my attacker via a video "I.D. parade." This is the long-distance equivalent of the police line-up: instead of fifteen similar-looking teenage boys lining up behind a pane of one-way glass, they've been video-taped for me to look at. The now-familiar nausea builds up in my stomach as I sit down to watch the I.D. parade – sweaty palms, heart palpitations, the urge to vomit at the mere thought of my attacker.

But then, when his face comes up on the screen, it's like a dart hitting the bull's eye. Bam! – that's him. No question about it. "It's Number Five," I tell the attending police officer with deceptive calm, as I nervously dent and un-dent my half-empty Diet Coke can.

Meanwhile, my gut turns inside me.

A few minutes later, while I'm decompressing with a friend in Starbucks, I get a text from another friend on sabbatical. She's on a volunteer mission with her boyfriend in Africa, and she's just gotten engaged.

I text her my congratulations, and then excuse myself from the coffee shop. After all, I have a hen party to attend in a number of hours. On the bus ride home, I'm shaking – either from the I.D. parade or the dread of attending this hen party, or both. Once home, I descend into tears, sobbing uselessly while fully aware that I'm supposed to be getting ready.

I have to get into a black dress. I have to wear heels. I have to put on make-up.

Is this for real? It feels like parallel worlds, moving from the I.D. parade of my rapist to a hen party. Or from giving my deposition to the police, the morning after my attack, to a red-carpet film premiere in Leicester Square. Are we really meant to be this versatile?

I show up almost two hours late to the hen party.

"Don't worry," Silvia winks at me, aware of my earlier visit to the Southwark Police Station. "You look great, anyway."

And the rest of that evening, I find myself drinking champagne and making mindless small talk, while underneath it all, my engine is working desperately, exhausted, struggling to keep up that façade.

*****

Silvia's wedding is in Slovakia that July, followed by another friend's in Dublin, and then another in Scotland that October. I am happy for all of them, of course, but having to dress up and maintain a certain cheery image becomes a superhuman chore for me. And then, of course, there is the envy. The sharp pain of watching my friends, surrounded by parents celebrating their marriage, pledging their mutual love with someone who is willing to be with them for the rest of their lives.

It's a cliché, but in the midst of it all, I feel very alone.

And as much as I try to avoid it, the questions and the self-doubt start to creep in. The lecture my parents might have given me, if they knew the truth. The speculation that maybe -- if I was just that little bit more conventional, if I was the kind of docile daughter of Chinese immigrants who went to medical school, who did what was expected, who allowed herself to be courted by some other Ivy League graduate, who wasn't still single at the age of twenty-nine, who didn't insist on backpacking solo through Europe, or going hiking alone in strange parks for fun -- maybe none of this would have ever happened.

But then again, if I was that person, I wouldn't have been me.

And however much I regret having gone into that park on that particular afternoon in Belfast, I still don't regret being who I am.

The old me would have found a certain solace in travel, so I follow that impulse, even though I am unsure what I can handle in my post-traumatic state. Whereas normally I would go somewhere remote, perhaps Third World, I decide to visit friends in the United States for all of August. Making my way from California, to Chicago, New York, and Boston, I find comfort in my friends – many of whom are settling into

57

different phases of their lives, getting engaged, starting new families.

On the last day of my trip, I find myself in Harvard Yard. There, I wander wistfully among the familiar greenery and slanting sunlight, the same dignified red-brick and grey stone buildings, which I haunted as an undergraduate ten years ago. I watch a few tourists, Asian parents proudly photographing their eight-year-olds on the Harvard campus, as if harbingers of their educational future. Everything seems eerily unchanged, even though I could not be farther from the inexperienced teenager I was when I came here.

After all, it was here where I learned that if you have talent, take charge, and strive for what you believe in, you can achieve anything. But they never told you that one day, when you least expect it, a random stranger can destroy your entire sense of self. Life is not always the meritocracy we want it to be. And that is not a lesson they teach you at Harvard.

But in this new, crueler reality, I am still trying to test my boundaries. I discover a budget airline sale and impulsively book a £22 return flight to Nîmes, in the South of France. This is the kind of thing I would have done before the attack – after all, there's a Roman aqueduct near the town that I've always wanted to see.

I consider it a challenge to the new, frightened me. So at some point in mid-October, I find myself checking into a small, family-owned hotel on my own. The hotel sits a stone's throw from the Roman arena, but in the off-season, it's eerie and completely empty, except for me -- and one other guest whom I never see, but hear once in a while. On top of that, the family who owns it is going away on vacation the evening I arrive. It's the perfect set-up for a horror movie, I think, as my post-traumatic panic starts to set in. That night, I push a chest of drawers in front of my door, before I crawl into my narrow bed and eventually fall into an uncomfortable sleep.

But the next morning, I find myself standing in front of the Pont du Gard: this ancient Roman aqueduct, rising like some ageless vision from the mist of the River Gardon. It towers over the otherwise empty valley, nearly two millennia old, and I find a certain constancy in the beauty of its massive, three-tiered presence. For a short while, I can almost forget the panic and unease which have been my constant companions since the attack. Just ancient stone, arching over tranquil waters.

On the hills above the Pont, various paths snake into the autumnal forest, and I start to explore them. My old excitement begins to stir. Part of me wants to go further down the path, discover more, see more – but then, the new fear sets in, snapping me back like a leash. The old me would have happily continued down that path, only too eager to explore beyond the next bend. The new me is cowardly, afraid of the unknown – and I turn back, defeated, to the safety of other tourists.

Once back in London, I realize I'm not really up to scratch. I must have been fooling myself to think I could travel on my own – and of course, work is out of the question. Besides, the production company I've run for the past six years has just been struck by the economic crisis and can no longer afford to pay my salary. My already modest income dwindles to nothing. And my career – until now, the driving force in my adulthood – is set adrift.

I sink into a tedious limbo. My hollowed-out shell collapses inwards, and becomes a negative void, dragging me down, like a black hole. After six months on the waiting list of the UK's National Health Service, I am finally assessed and diagnosed with Post-Traumatic Stress Disorder. I am prescribed fifteen sessions of Cognitive Behaviour Therapy at the Centre for Anxiety Disorders and Trauma. They are exhausting, and involve endless sets of questionnaires, asking how many times I've had nightmares each week, how many times I've panicked.

But these dark winter months are dominated by the slow ticking of the clock, the inevitable drag towards the moment I have long been dreading – the moment when I take to the stand to testify against my attacker in court. The Belfast police give me what information they can, but by now, the case is in the hands of the Public Prosecution Service, working its way through the bureaucratic processes of the Northern Irish judicial system. I know my attacker has been held in a juvenile detention center since a week after my assault, and that he has been pleading not guilty. Beyond that, I am told little else, other than that at some point early next year, I must fly back to Belfast to testify in court.

Eventually, the date is set for the 8th of March 2009.

And so, my entire life becomes a slow, fearful countdown to that dreaded date. Proxy Me flies to Los Angeles to spend a joyless, unmemorable Christmas and New Year's with my parents, who are still unaware of what happened. Other than that, I am mainly confined to a grey, anxious existence in London, pulled so taut with nerves over the impending court date, that I find it impossible to relax, or enjoy anything.

I finally decide to go on anti-depressants. On the advice of my psychologist, I start going to the gym regularly. I take up Buddhist meditation. I play Brickbreaker on my BlackBerry. A lot. Anything to calm me down even slightly from this unrelenting anxiety. But the tension is magnified in my nightmares, and the thought of seeing him in court makes me sick to my stomach.

And yet, I am aware that my nervousness is some heightened version of the tension I felt as a child, in the minutes leading up to a piano recital. The expectation to perform. To not screw up. Even while describing, in detail, in public, the ordeal of my rape, while sitting across from my attacker.

Even now, we can't escape our high expectations. Our exacting definition of success. Will I perform to the best of my abilities in court? That is the question which plagues me the most as the 8th of March draws near.

Am I up to it? It's not about him, and it's not about the rape itself. It's about me.

*****

And then, on the morning of the 8th of March, in a courthouse near Belfast – everything changes within minutes. Waiting for the jury to be selected, I sit with my friends in a separate room, nearly sick to my stomach. I am suddenly told that he has pleaded guilty at the last minute.

"So....there won't be a trial?" I ask, disbelieving. "I don't have to testify?

And just like that, my most dreaded moment suddenly vanishes. The whole purpose of my trip to Belfast, the cause of all my months of anxiety is suddenly negated. It feels anticlimactic – and completely surreal.

My friends are jubilant, and I'm flooded with relief. But part of me – perhaps the competitive side of me -- feels partially robbed of a showdown, of the chance to actually confront the boy who brought on my past year of misery, and to see justice be done.

Six weeks later, I do get that chance when I'm back in Belfast for the sentencing hearing. This is the final step in the judicial process, and while I am not required to attend, I feel that I want to see this through to the very end. I had set this process in motion the moment I decided to contact the police that afternoon – and to not forget the attack had happened. And now, more than a year later, I would see that process finally completed.

In the meantime, I've fallen ill for the past six weeks, sleeping fifteen hours a day, while my body starts the long journey of recovering from a year of constant anxiety, PTSD, and depression. A friend holds my hand as I sit in court that day, and I'm aware of my attacker's family sitting in the same row, ten seats away.

Then, the judge enters the room. We listen as he sentences my attacker (now sixteen-years-old) to eight years in prison. There is a very clinical, mathematical explanation of how he calculated eight years, based on judicial precedent and the particulars of the case. The police detective next to me remarks that this is a more severe sentence than he had expected. And then the hearing is over.

My attacker's family gathers around their son, who has been sitting in the dock until now. He's just been sentenced for half the length of his current lifetime. Just once, I see him turn his head and look at me, but I don't lock eyes with him. It's over. I do not need to see more. I only want to look ahead from now on.

That evening, my friend and I decide to drink a bottle of champagne while waiting for our flight back to London. Once aboard, we order another half-bottle from the in-flight menu. By the time we're halfway through the flight, we are both roaring drunk. Several of the other passengers, look back at us – but I could care less. This is the first time I've been able to enjoy champagne in over a year. And by God, do I have a reason to celebrate.

*****

Less than two days later, I'm on another budget flight, this time all by myself to Croatia. I've wanted to visit Croatia for years, and now with the completion of the judicial process, all my previous fears about traveling have miraculously been lifted.

I haven't even booked any accommodation, but when I step off the bus in Split, I find myself bargaining with an old man for a private room in the Old Town. My six days in Croatia flash by in a stream of sun-spangled beach and

Mediterranean architecture. I marvel at Diocletian's Palace in Split, sun myself on the deck of a ferry, scramble atop the city walls of Dubrovnik. I'm on my own, but that shadow of fear which haunted me in Nîmes is gone in the clarity of the Mediterranean sun.

Nor do I stop there. Emboldened by my rediscovered ability to travel, I join some American friends for a trip to Vietnam and Cambodia. I add on a weeklong stopover in Borneo, just for myself. I watch orangutans in awe, snorkel through tropical waters, bond with other backpackers over late-night card games in the middle of the jungle.

Even weddings become gradually more enjoyable for me. I have five to attend that year, in various countries. But with each subsequent wedding, the once-brittle shell version of me is filling out, turning solid and real once more. For the first time in a very long time, I have something to be proud of – the fact that I fulfilled my responsibility as a rape victim, and I've done it well, putting my attacker behind bars. Things would only get better from here.

But not instantaneously. My recovery is gradual. While travel increasingly makes me feel more like the old me, it's not the same in London. Various forms of therapy – physical, holistic, psychological – continue, and I still constantly feel ill and exhausted.

The thought of work doesn't even cross my mind. I fill out the occasional job application, but why work now, when I can enjoy life? When I haven't been able to enjoy life in ages?

Even before the attack, I'd been so dedicated to the notion of working hard, of achieving success (however I chose to define it), that life itself- when I wasn't travelling – was constantly determined by expectations, accomplishments, obligations.

Now with my attacker sentenced, I realized my only obligations were to myself – to recover and heal. To become the person I wanted to be again, maybe even stronger than before. I felt that if I could survive the last twelve months, and handle that on my own, then I could survive almost anything.

So would I eventually piece together my professional life and somehow resume a meaningful career?

Yes, I would.

Would I one day have the kind of personal and family life I envisioned?

I hoped so.

But I had the whole rest of my life to figure that out, and I knew I could trust myself to perform to the best of my abilities, when the time came.

So for now, I felt I deserved a little time off.

I spent the last three months of 2009 backpacking on my own through Southeast Asia. After my trip to Vietnam in the spring, I realized how easy it was to travel in that part of the world, even how comforting it was to blend in visually, and not to look so obviously foreign. So I booked a cheap flight from London to Bangkok and back, with three months in between (the maximum stay). I wasn't really sure where I'd go during this time, but I knew I'd be able to improvise as I went along.

The day I landed in Bangkok, *The Belfast Telegraph* printed my anonymous article about my experience as a foreigner, randomly attacked and raped while traveling in Belfast. As I sat on the Khao San Road, enjoying a Pad Thai and a Beer Chang, and reading a downloaded scan of the article on my BlackBerry, I wondered if any readers of that article would expect I'd be here, about to start a three-month backpacking trip, all on my own.

I smiled as the thought crossed my mind. I'd done my part. I'd been through the worst of it and back, and lived to tell the tale. And here I was, at the start of a new journey, reading my own article in print. Since childhood, I'd always wanted to be a professional writer, but I'd been deterred when my parents warned me how un-lucrative that job was, how unpredictable.

But what wasn't unpredictable? Six months ago, when I was agonizing about the trial of my rapist, would I have predicted that in September I'd be here, eager to embark on a solo backpacking trip for three months? And twelve months before that, would I have predicted that one spring afternoon in Belfast, I would be assaulted and raped while walking through a park?

Life moves in capricious circles like that, doubling back upon itself, betraying the ground beneath you. You can have your plans and your expectations, but you never know what waits around the next bend. The best you can do is to live in the moment, and to follow your instincts, if the going gets tough. Sometimes you get lost, and sometimes you don't have a map. But most of the time, you don't need one – you learn to trust yourself.

Winnie Li (http://winniemli.com) is a writer and filmmaker. She has achieved multiple accolades for her films, including an Oscar nomination. A former writer for the *Let's Go* travel guide books, Winnie has traveled extensively on five continents. She is currently aiming to finish her comedic first novel, *Fag Hag and Other Fairy Tales*. A Taiwanese-American raised in New Jersey, she worked for Ugly Duckling Films in London for nearly 9 years and now works for the Doha Tribeca Film Festival and Doha Film Institute in Qatar. In April 2011 three years after the attack, she hiked the 95-mile West Highland Way in Scotland, on her own.

Random Musings

By Bava Wadhwa

Self help books often emphasize the importance of conscious living: conscious breathing to improve the state of one's mental and physical health, conscious eating to improve the absorption of the food's nutrients, conscious being to appreciate and enjoy the going-ons in your living environment.

Bava's musings made me a little more conscious of and sensitive to the moment – good for the heart, good for the mind and certainly good for the soul. Enjoy. - *Ed*

~ 7 ~

Venus and Vindaloo

venus and vindaloo
a heady combination
attractive to the new and a few

garam masalas
roman piazzas
funny clothing
croissants in the morning

venus vindaloo
a burning planet
for me and who?

on clear nights
after lips and bites
in my supine state
her light penetrates; ameliorates

venus@vindaloo
eyes are red
the soul is blue

love and spice
cum at a high price
exotic aromas, lingering and tantric
burning taste buds, numbed but frantic

venus and vindaloo
clinging under
an Indian moon

*****

Mourning in Hull

I walk down a hill littered with cigarettes and refuse
The air is furious and cold
Sparrows can be heard from near and far
It's morning on my way to Hull
The people line up single file
The nicest Canadians you ever did see
No pushing, no jostling, "after you", a free newspaper
The bus-stop on a Friday morning in Hull

Today I don't get a seat
Bouncing and bumping we traverse the river
The resigned faces of the public
Servants to the clock
During morning in Hull

This place is exactly like the next
Indistinguishable cubicles between,
the front, the sides and the behind
back and around
Yet, a few nice corners lined with plants
Turning their face
To morning in Hull

Sitting here in my fabric walls
My screen a link to the virtual world
I contemplate another day of work
Craning my neck for inspiration
From morning in Hull

And now the people are slowly filtering in
The tapping of the keys gets louder and more frequent
Sounds and movement are beginning to change
Until another morning in Hull

*****

The Possibilities are Endless

thermal underwear
hot hot hot

a climbing harness
to hold you in spot
indiglo alarm clock
beeps at cold dawn
moisture wicking
nexus-backed tegralatex

oooh

i like
u lock
with an oversized case
and dark metal block
swix glide wax
cork polish scrape

an altimetre, barometer, electronic compass
with declination adjustment
monitoring the climax rate

*****

Midas Touch

Sometimes Love
Is the colour of bruises

Purple passion
Black affection
Blue legacy

All these marks
Get set
Now go

Baljit Wadhwa, or Bava as she is known to her family and friends, was born in Canada to Indian parents. She studied Molecular Biology at the University of Calgary and Natural Resource Management at the University of Waterloo. An irresistible desire for adventure took her to five cities in ten years, and in 2006 she moved to Washington D.C. to work on sustainable public and private sector investment. Bava currently works to evaluate international environmental projects but, given the choice, would spend more of her time indulging in her gear fetish, paddling or taking photos while watching the world go by.

To Be or Not to Be...

By Isabel Hagbrink

"To be or not to be"? Ubiquitous as this phrase has become, for many women, it is a very real question. To be one's authentic self? To be as others expect? To dilute or hide certain qualities so as to be(come) more 'desirable'? Is there a smart way? Is there a right way? As we get older, wiser and more confident in who we are, we also move onto ground that is at once more solid, and yet shakier. Why shakier? Because of the ticking biological clock. The lingering fear that one may forever remain a childless spinster. And all because of the desire to have a career and a family at the same time. Of wanting to be seen and heard but not to create so much shadow and noise that our lovers become uncomfortable and choose to be with someone "less" instead. Less forward. Less active. Less independent.

Isabel's dilemma is probably shared by many of us. A modern woman with a career, she questions whether her fun, feisty personality—indeed her best qualities—are the reason why the dream of a life partner (not to be confused with the desire to 'have a man' but, rather, the longing for a co-conspirator in the best of senses) remains elusive. - *Ed*

~ *8* ~

So it has come to this: *I'd be a better date if I were a man.* My friend Faith tells me one day, and I believe her: "*You'd make a great husband!*" Not sure if I should take this as a compliment. Her comment doesn't bode well for my dating game since straight guys aren't usually looking for 'great husband' types...

The thing is it's not really my fault. It's Mom's. She apparently raised me to be a great potential hubbie – a proactive, organized, resourceful and well-traveled person who knows how to weather-proof windows, assembles IKEA furniture in a jiffy, is on first-name basis with the folks in the local hardware store, and is financially independent to boot.

I'm not sure when it all started. But growing up with an independent mother who whisked me around the world from the tender age of nine probably had something to do with it. I loved meeting new people and cultures, and became an adventurer, whether I liked it or not. And it's been that way ever since.

In my twenties, this meant taking off to Venezuela to write a thesis and do odd jobs. In my thirties, I worked with aid programs in the Caribbean. Nowadays, as I have more or less settled in Washington D.C., it means that I'm the eternal local explorer, always on the look-out for romantic getaways and cozy new restaurants. Catching the latest artsy flick and finding nearby farms to pick pumpkins for Halloween. Friends from near and far call for advice on what to do and where to go. Newbies in town ask if they can tag along and I am always happy to take them, if they can keep up!

It doesn't stop there. I have quirky personal guides to all my favorite cities from Barcelona to Miami, Stockholm to Tokyo. God forbid friends should visit Kenya and miss the best little leather shop in Nairobi for that perfect cow hide clutch. Whatever the need or question, call Isabel. I could give you ideas for a great date night in at least 10 countries. And if I don't know the answer, I know someone who does.

Unfortunately, there is a downside to these strengths, especially where dating is involved. It's tough to take Isabel out in town to show her something new. I have to hold back when a guy asks if I have been to that new Japanese restaurant downtown that everyone is raving about, because of course I have. I hate to show my disappointment when the most romantic suggestion for Valentine's is dinner and a movie; I could have thought of so many more exciting things to do. A male friend recently asked me, a bit in awe of everything I did: "How does a man keep you interested?"

I think men feel a tad emasculated. Some years ago, my then boyfriend told me, as he followed me into the street in Cuzco to find a taxi at 6am - late for the train to Macchu Picchu - that *"dating you is like dating a man"*. So, Faith isn't the only one to notice. Some Peruvians, it seems, are not used to women hailing their own early morning rides either. But after surviving Hurricane George in a flooded apartment in Santo Domingo and getting on with no electricity for weeks, hailing a cab just doesn't seem like a big deal.

I have a friend in Sweden who remarked last summer that he wants to be with a woman he can take under his wing and show the world. He specifically does not want to be with someone who has seen more places around the world than he has. This surprises me as I've always assumed that emancipated Swedish men, in particular, would prefer a woman who can hold her own and carry it too. Of course, different courses for different horses, but what on Earth does this mean for a gal like me?

Realizing that a man is more attracted to the damsel in distress than to Miss Independent, has been cause for plenty of self-doubt and frustration over the last few years. In my twenties, for example, I had no problem rejecting macho men who appeared to feel threatened by me. I readily dismissed them and their insecurities, happy to wait for someone more mature to come along, confident that my 'ideal man' was just around the proverbial corner.

These days however, I increasingly wonder if I might have been following the wrong recipe for love. That perhaps being myself – strong and savvy – and remaining true to my character, is not the best strategy for snagging a man.

I never agreed with the love advice touted in books such as *The Rules,* but I have started to wonder if showing the full strength of my personality early in the relationship is akin to shooting myself in the foot, relationship-wise that is. Should I tone down my personality, at least in the initial phase of a romance? Should I do what I can to boost his ego, let him believe he is right, rather than to point out a mistake? For example, if a man takes the wrong turn when driving, do you keep mum or pipe up? I would instinctively let him know, but a lot of my girlfriends would not. Let him be, they'd say, he is the one driving the car.

Meryl Streep wrote in her contribution to Katie Couric's book *'The Best Advice I Ever Got'*, that it took her years to find her true voice. When she did, it wasn't the demure, pretty, softly giggling woman whom she tried on for size as a teenager and whom all the men fell for. That was just an act. Her true temperament, she says, developed later in life – when she became the slightly bossy, opinionated, loud and high-spirited woman she is today. And it scared men off – although it clearly hasn't hampered her career.

I identify with most of those traits she discovered in herself. It's ironic that qualities that make women successful at work are the same things that keep us in long-term singlehood. In order to keep a relationship going, is it possible that strong women must turn off these qualities? Do we need to start tap dancing around men, censoring what we say to make sure that egos are not bruised and using positive reinforcement to make them feel that they are in charge?

What is interesting is that strong men are almost always initially attracted to strong, confident women. At least that is what they tell us. One of the first things that suitors gush about is just how much they're taken by my joie-de-vivre. However, after a few months, things inevitably change. When we remain active, full of ideas, opinionated, and willing to stand up for what we think is right, they start to back off.

I remember an ex-boyfriend telling me, *"I compete all day at work; I don't want to compete at home."* What brought on the comment I can no longer recall – probably some silly discussion on where to hang a painting in our home – but it hit a nerve.

The solution for many women who share my dilemma has been to hold back and pretend to be less than they truly are 100% of the time. To let a man make the calls, take the decisions, be the one who drives the relationship, is to preserve that unseen Maginot line of male territory over which we ladies must not stray. I had a friend who asked me: "Would you rather be right or happy?" implying that many a fight is not worth having. If you are always trying to prove a point, you're engaged in being right instead of being engaged in the relationship, they say. There is a lot of truth in this. A relationship is all about compromise. But *don't sweat the small stuff* is a difficult lesson to learn, especially for Type A personalities.

Most of my female friends battle with this case of split personality daily. They 'take charge' and are successful women at work, but switch off and become less pro-active in their more personal relationships. These women run companies but pretend that they can't make dinner reservations.

"Let him be the one to make the plans, don't show him you're too interested, don't take his every call. Play hard to get because men like to chase and they don't want to get a girl who comes to them too easily," is the kind of well-meaning advice I've heard time and again. But is this really a viable solution? How long must I sustain it? Would this become a life-long pretense or would I go back to my old self when, and if, I marry?

In my years living in Latin America, I saw this scenario played out over and over: Sweet, passive girl marries strong, aggressive man who has chased her for years. After the ring is on the fourth finger, she suddenly shows her true colors and rules the family with an iron fist. But deep in my Swedish soul, I feel that not showing my genuine personality would be the worst kind of dishonesty. I couldn't don a cloak of passivity and play a game of hard-to-get solely for the sake of *'catching'* a man. For the longest time, I have held on to the belief that the one who is out there for me will want me just the way I am, without subterfuges and deceptions. Feisty, yes! Stubborn, sure! But I'm really a romantic at heart.

It seems the interaction between men and women, however, is an ancient dance that has remained unchanged in the 21st century. A man's instinct is to pursue and conquer a woman. No matter how rational or in tune with modern times we say we are. No matter how much men assure us that they like women being direct and forthcoming. This is simply not the case. Any female who does not abide by the rules of this game makes it that much harder for herself in trying to *get* the man.

That last realization comes from a hard-learned lesson. Once I was in a serious relationship with a difficult, traditional man and, consequently, adjusted my personality to fit his. To avoid upsetting him, I stopped chatting to people in the grocery store and repressed my curious, bubbly personality. Eventually, it got to be more than I could handle and I broke it off. Sometime later, when he attempted to rekindle our relationship, I refused, knowing that I did not like the timid wall flower I had become while with him.

But where does that leave women like me? Our mothers were pioneers in breaking the mold *and* the glass ceiling, yet *we* are the first generation of women expecting, and who are expected, to have it all. We have shown that we are the equals of men – we can get a great education and a respectable job - so why is it so hard to achieve the happy home life too? We've been told to reach for the sky but developing the personality needed for a successful career seems actually to become an obstacle to a long-lasting relationship. Many of my more open minded male friends will tell me I am exaggerating, but I am sorry to say that I speak from experience.

Ultimately my experiences have answered the important question: Can I play the game? The answer is no, I can't play it well or, at least, maintain it for long. I have discovered that as frustrated as I am about being single, I would rather embrace the lonely state than be stuck in a role that smothers and makes me resent both my partner and myself. Centuries ago, Shakespeare, who knew a thing or two about human nature, said:

"This above all: to thine own self be true. It must follow that you cannot then be false to any man."

His words were not written to reflect modern relationships, but are apt. It boils down to this: Maybe it's a good idea to tone it down a notch or two in your relationship with a man, especially if you're typically quite critical. We can all strive to be kinder and gentler, to be more patient and accepting of people. But we mustn't play games or assume roles that are not in line with who we are, that we do not feel natural and comfortable with, because sooner or later that lack of comfort will be the ruin of anything good we might lay claim to in a relationship.

So, what does the future hold for me in love and life? Only time will tell. After every failed relationship I feel like throwing in the towel and protecting my shredded, aching heart. Giving up on men entirely. Having kids on my own, as some of my beautiful, independent and strong women friends have done. But then I meet a wonderful guy, things brighten up and I decide to give it another go, all the while remaining true to who I am and what I want...and that I'd rather wait than be anyone other than myself.

Isabel Hagbrink was born in Sweden. Her mother being a diplomat, she globe trotted a fair bit, living in Poland and Pakistan before going to boarding school in Sweden. Isabel studied finance and economics at the Stockholm School of Economics, and received a Masters Degree in International Relations from Johns Hopkins University/SAIS in Washington D.C. She has worked at the Inter-American Development Bank in project finance and in external communications, as well as in the private sector with projects that reduce greenhouse gas emissions. Isabel lives in Washington D.C., where she is presently the Senior Communications Officer of the World Bank's Carbon Finance Unit. On any given evening, you'll find her biking around the city, enjoying the warm breeze of adventure, small or big.

Leadership Reflections

By Swaady Martin-Leke

So much has been written about the topic of leadership that one can conclude that there is no fixed formula to becoming a leader. True leadership is very much a unique set of behaviors and values, evolved from an individual's DNA and adapted to the needs of the situation. While it is challenging to define, it is not difficult to recognize good leadership when we see it and, to feel it instantly when there is a void in the same.

Swaady is an attractive and petite lady who possesses an iron will and boundless energy, unfettered by the 'bling' of her career successes to date. Through her reflections on what it takes to make a difference, we get a glimpse of how she is translating experiences into an ambition to shape the Continent she is from. She could have easily opted to escape the challenges and erase the ugly memories of her past, but has not. Rather she has chosen to confront many of the issues that wrought her own childhood. That, to me, is a mark of courage and the symbol of a leader. - *Ed*

- 9 -

"Come to the edge, he said. They said, we are afraid. Come to the edge, he said. They came, he pushed them, and they flew."

Guillaume Apollinaire

12th of April 1980: President W. Tolbert of Liberia was brutally murdered in a military coup by Master Sergeant Samuel Doe, a 28 year old illiterate. A few days later, Tolbert's cabinet members were publicly executed. They were tied to poles on a beach in the capital, Monrovia, and shot. Subsequently, Doe suspended the constitution and took over power. This coup started a vicious circle of violence, instability and impoverishment: a descent into hell familiar to many Africans.

I was about 3 years old then, and my family had settled in Liberia six years before. The fears, the tears: the night's silence was often interrupted by random shots and screams. We hid under the beds, terrorized, clinging to each other and breathing shallowly to make no noise. In our imagination, vandals were bursting into the house, ripping us out of our hiding places to torture and kill whoever they found. Day after day, night after night, we played the same movie in our heads.

Yet, in the midst of this uncertainty my life was punctuated by a well-organized schedule of meals, silent plays and naps. The smile and love of my mother was my sky and my world.

As soon as the airport reopened, my family fled Monrovia, leaving everything behind – including my father – and finding refuge in Senegal, where my mother had some family. For a year we lived at my uncle's before emigrating to Côte d'Ivoire to start a new life.

What do you remember when you are only 3 years old and pushed to the very edge of life?

Memories are blurry, scattered in the labyrinths of unconsciousness. My child brain has locked the fears and horrors of civil war somewhere very deep from where they cannot re-surface. There are images but the sequences cannot be traced back. What remains vivid are the consequences and the impact such events have had on my life.

*****

18th of December 2009: Almost 30 years after the Liberian coup and slightly older than Doe when he overthrew Tolbert, I now live in South Africa. I am one of only a few regional female leaders at General Electric, one of the world's largest companies, and I have just signed a landmark contract between the company and the South African national railway to supply one hundred locomotives. This is one of the largest contracts GE has signed to date on the African continent. In the process of fulfilling this, we will help South Africa and Africa as a whole both make a technological leap in infrastructure building and also strengthen local skills.

Our African collective history is filled with countless lost futures, wasted childhoods and brutal passages into adulthood. Ten years ago, I had accepted my first job at GE as an internal auditor for the Consumer Finance division. To go from the ashes of civil war in Liberia to a regional leadership role in GE, I had to decide whether to look at life as a glass half empty or half full. Whether to let the traumas of such human tragedy haunt and drag me down, or to choose to overcome them.

I am a self-motivated optimist. I work hard, and give the best I can. I don't expect anything from anyone, whether in life or my career. If I am not satisfied with a situation, I will either deal with it, fix it, or walk away for better shores.

I remember that I was once a refugee. My life would never be the same. I felt un-rooted, relentlessly looking for "home", a precious treasure that cannot be taken for granted. After traveling the world, living in more than 10 different countries in 30 years, I realize that you can never find home in a place. It is within you, and I have carried it with me all along.

"Home" is your soul.

*****

This knowledge grounds me and helps me put things in perspective. Too many times, we give undue importance to

81

things which don't really matter in the bigger scheme of things of life. Would that injustice experienced in the workplace really matter if we were about to die? And, so, going back to the essentials of life, what matters, is vital if you want to maintain your sanity in a ruthless corporate world.

Destiny is a dice. You throw as best as you can, and then take responsibility for the outcome. You will never fully understand why your fortune has been different from that of your neighbor. You were the same age and had the same promising future, but her family only escaped 15 years into the conflict. With no resources, she was never able to complete her education and went on to be a refugee in Côte d'Ivoire. She scraped a living juggling several jobs. She died last month for lack of healthcare, 300 km away from Abidjan.

I escaped and went on to a life full of unexpected opportunities and great successes. I am humbled and grateful. Every success is a blessing. And every failure is an opportunity to learn. Learn and move on quickly!

I learned that material things don't matter, as everything you have can disappear overnight. The villa we once lived in faded into one room shared with my mum and brother. The toys I once accumulated were burned to ashes in a second. Material things are ephemeral: they don't determine your value as a human being. I will never search for riches nor let them define me, but I seek constantly to enrich my soul. Whether struggling to make ends meet or earning a big executive salary, my inner peace and happiness is not shaken.

I am free.

*****

I discover that hope and faith can never be lost. Left behind, my father would live through a series of civil wars in Liberia, Guinea, Nigeria and Sudan. I corresponded with him for a few years, then lost sight of him for two decades. For 20 years, I prayed that I would not die before I saw him again: and then one day, miraculously, I found him. The love and connection between us had remained intact.

I have become a knower, not anymore a believer. I would never lose sleep over planning life or career. I have an end-goal and a direction, but I find it helpful to remain constantly open to change and embrace it when it knocks at my door.

Nothing is constant but change. And change can be a beautiful thing.

*****

Like so many other such leaders, Doe failed us Africans: he failed his people, his country and his continent. He failed to step up to his responsibility, the responsibility of making a positive contribution to our history and people. How could a young African leader throw his country and people into such chaos, chaos that would end only 25 years later when Africa elected its first ever female head of state: Ellen Johnson-Sirleaf?

Yet the same country that produced Doe also produced Sirleaf – the two leaders could not be any more different. Through Sirleaf's leadership, national hope has been revived, Liberia's reputation and credibility have been restored, and tremendous progress has been made in achieving development goals.

Sirleaf is passionately committed to the cause, deeply grounded on strong moral and humanist values. There is no doubt that her empowering and participative leadership, as well as her genuine interest for her people, has helped turn Liberia around and raise the nation.

How many other Sirleafs can Africa produce – women who would change the destiny of a nation and a continent? Women who are great thinkers, great innovators, great entrepreneurs, great achievers and great leaders?

I recognize that the importance of leadership cannot be underplayed, as one's future depends greatly on one's leaders. One person can change the course of your life and who you become. I seek to become a true leader – someone who motivates, inspires, empowers and, above all, serves others with unyielding integrity. I am purposeful. What matters is the cause, not me. I will not indulge in self-pity.

My parents never encouraged bitterness, resentment nor helplessness for any of the dramas of Africa and its bad leaders. On the contrary, they challenged me to be part of the solution. The continent will not change if we, as Africans, are not making this change happen. We have no alternative but to work towards positive transformation with determination.

Through my upbringing, they helped me build an unwavering confidence in myself and a deep sense of purpose grounded in spirituality. They were advocates of the "African Renaissance" and Pan-Africanism. My brother and I were raised on stories of great African leaders such as Soundjata Keita and Kwame N'Krumah. They made sure we had a strong sense of "African-ness" and "African pride". They nurtured a resilient consciousness of the role we must play within the bigger scheme of things, and especially in Africa.

"When you are born African, you are born with a responsibility," my dad would say. This message stuck with me throughout the years, and my life choices have subsequently always been very intuitive. There was never a doubt in my mind that I would come back to Africa to be an agent of positive change. I set up my life objectives at a very young age, and these have never changed.

It was always about transforming my continent.

*****

When I started my career at GE, the Global CEO of the division invited me to his office for a 15-minute mentoring session. He left me with a piece of advice which shaped my career: "Always do something you are passionate about. This is the only way to excel in whatever you are doing."

Finding your passion is like falling madly in love. I am passionately in love with Africa, and this helps me go through the challenges of corporate life. I have been ready to accept all the hardships that come with it, but I never compromise on the end-goal: making a positive impact in Africa. Whether it is in what I do – working on sustainable infrastructure building, skills development, technology transfer, women's empowerment, environmental conservation, education at large – or by developing myself as a positive role model for those around me, the focus remains the same: a better Africa for all.

Today there are less than 10 women heads of state out of 195 countries. In the private sector, only one percent of the CEOs of the world's top 500 companies are women. In Africa, this number is probably reduced by more than half. It is also very obvious at regional and international gatherings that women are always in the minority. Organizers of events struggle to bring diversity to the panels and participants. Whether in the public or private sector, the low representation of women in leadership positions remains an issue.

As women, we must make use of whatever experience we face throughout our life, positive or negative, to propel ourselves to higher grounds where we will make a lasting and impactful difference. How are these experiences shaping us as leaders? How will we get rid of the fear of failure – the sense that we cannot make it to the top? Sometimes being pushed off the edge creates the opportunity for us to fly.

Swaady Martin-Leke, a native of Côte d'Ivoire and France, is the founder & CEO of eco-luxury Africa tea company, KYI SWAARA. Prior to launching her own venture, she spent most of her career at General Electric, where she developed the company's first strategic plans or "GrowthPlaybooks" for the Africa region. As a strong advocate of women's empowerment, she led the re-launch of the GE Women's Network in Africa, which focuses on women helping women to excel through various initiatives focused on leadership, advancement and career-broadening opportunities. Swaady holds a Master's Degree in Economic Sciences from the University of Lausanne, Switzerland. In 2011, she was named "New Leader of the Future" by the Forum of Crans Montana. She lives in South Africa with her husband, Acha.

Three Women in My Life

By Maya Horii

Three people, one is a teacher – Confucius.

In my multiple encounters with friends, colleagues, acquaintances and strangers, I am reminded, time and again, that there is always something to learn from another person, no matter his or her station in life. The elements infused, whether conscious and deliberate or subtle and subliminal, and whether in the form of a comment or an action, become influences which makes us who we are today. Once in a while, someone leaves a distinctive mark that we reflect upon regularly and use as a guiding light to navigate our lives.

Maya's story speaks of the inspiring influences in her life, reminding us of the many people who we have crossed paths with and for whom we can be thankful. - *Ed*

~ 10 ~

Although I did not come to appreciate this until I was fairly grown-up, my family was more externally-oriented and internationally-minded than the average family in Japan. My father, a typical 'salary man,' was a civil engineer and spent much of his professional life in the 1970s and 1980s working in the Middle East and Southeast Asia; it was a time when Japanese construction companies were leading many new development projects of ports and harbors around the world.

My mother took care of me and my brother at home, but nonetheless had a small global experience of her own – she taught Japanese in a language school to students from abroad and befriended American, European and Asian scholars who were visiting the national university in our town. At least once a year, she invited students and friends to our home, delighting visitors with home-made food, putting the girls in kimonos and taking dozens of photographs of everyone.

And so it was that I grew up curious about the outside world. At my elementary school graduation, every child gave an almost obligatory one-sentence statement after receiving their diploma. Most asserted things like "I will work hard in English and math classes when I start middle school" or "I will make a lot of friends in the new middle school I'm attending," I remember saying, "I want to make a difference in the world by working internationally and helping people."

*****

My first exposure to someone with an experience of seeing the world was my ballet teacher, Yoko Ichino, who came to our studio for the summer and winter as a guest instructor. I was about ten years old then. Yoko and her husband, David Nixon, were principal dancers at the National Ballet of Canada at that time, and appeared as guest artists in Europe and U.S. (Today, they are the Ballet Mistress and the Artistic Director of the Northern Ballet Theatre in England).

Yoko-sensei taught our ballet classes; Nixon-san choreographed pieces for our summer recitals. I practiced English ceaselessly so that I could talk to them. Yoko-sensei was always bursting with energy and had an endearing smile. She demanded a lot from her students, but was also surprisingly positive and encouraging. As far as I can remember, that was the first time growing up that I had received encouragement. Because of Yoko, I learned to love working hard and was happy to be in the upbeat environment of our ballet class all day long in the heat of summer.

One day, after several hours of rehearsals, Yoko-sensei showed us a video of students at the Canada's National Ballet School performing the exact same piece that she and Nixon-san had choreographed for us the previous summer. As I saw the beautiful blonde, tall and slim girls perform the piece that we thought was 'ours', tears began to roll down my cheeks uncontrollably. Mixed emotions of jealousy and envy for these talented students who were able to spend their time on ballet, and a realization that I was never going to be good enough overwhelmed me. Yoko-sensei pulled me aside and told me, *"If you believe in what you are passionate about, and you love what you do, it doesn't matter where you come from and what you look like. I know you dance with your heart, and that is what's important"* –these words from a world-class ballerina have made me focus on what I am passionate about to this day.

*****

By the time I started high school, I became increasingly frustrated by the fact that, even though Japan was ranked as the world's second largest economy (at least, until recently), our leaders, both in the political and business arenas, had very little presence on the global stage. Japanese companies – Toyota, SONY, Nintendo to name a few –, may be well known around the world, but no single manager at or near their helm appeared charismatic or influential enough to stand head-to-head with other global leaders at an individual level. I concluded that this was the result of a largely passive and reactive education system that focused on rote learning and did not cultivate a students' ability to problem-solve, communicate and express themselves, especially in English.

When I was seventeen, motivated by a drive to see the world outside of Tokyo, I left home for a year on an exchange program to live with a French-American family in San Diego. It was the first time I had experienced life in America and it was full of new discoveries and learnings. At the same time, I grew to better appreciate the surroundings in Japan – public transportation that allowed me to go everywhere on my own, and the almost universal service hospitality of stores and restaurants. After returning home and finishing high school, I received an offer to attend both the University of Tokyo, one of the most prestigious schools in Japan, and Harvard College in the United States. I ended up spending 5 months at the University of Tokyo after high school graduation in March, meeting many friends and even joining the cheerleading squad, before leaving for Harvard in the Fall of 1998.

*****

While I was a third year student at Harvard, my professor of Japanese Politics introduced me to Dr. Sadako Ogata, then the United Nations High Commissioner for Refugees, at a dinner that honored her accomplishments within the organization. Dr. Ogata became the agency's Head in 1991, and handled various crises from human rights issues in Kosovo to Rwandan refugee camps. A small, soft-spoken Japanese woman, yet quietly determined and strong, she gained respect from people around the world for tackling the most difficult challenges of her time – saving the lives of millions of refugees while maintaining neutrality to the conflicts and evolving political events.

In person, Dr. Ogata was even more petite than I had expected, but her conviction and humor made me feel that she could singularly pave the way for our generation. When my professor introduced me to her, she said, *"You have already accomplished so much to be able to study at Harvard, and there is endless opportunity ahead of you. You should try anything you want to do, without being scared of what mistakes you would make or what others would think of you."* That became my second mantra.

*****

After college, I found my passion while working in Indonesia and Philippines. I had my first direct exposure to the world of foreign aid, often witnessing first-hand how things do not work, especially due to the lack of capability and attention to project management. I decided to pursue a degree in economic development at the Kennedy School of Government to better understand the workings of

90

government. Together with 65 other classmates representing more than twenty-five countries, I had a true opportunity to learn from friends from all over the world, and immerse myself into understanding international development.

As the end of the program approached, there was a question of what I would do afterwards. My mother very much wanted me to pursue a Ph.D. She has been supporting me all these years through my obsession with ballet, decision to participate in an exchange program, and leave home for college in the U.S. In some sense, I think she lived part of her own dreams through the freedom that I was afforded – seeing the world was not a luxury that many in her generation enjoyed. In return, I have always tried to live up to her expectations and be a good daughter - do well in everything I did, from school to ballet to other after school lessons.

As a professor in a Japanese university without a doctorate, my mother knew more than anyone else how having a complete set of credentials was key in the then (and still now!) male-dominated academia. While it is true that my mother managed to successfully find her own way into a university teaching position, eventually heading up a department for Japanese language instruction, she always felt she could have achieved more had she furthered her education.

I thought hard about the decision – despite my mother's advice, my love for working with people to make tangible changes did not seem consistent with spending another few years in research to pursue a PhD. I wrote my mother a long email to explain. It was serendipitous that, just as I hit the 'send' button, a note arrived from her – it read *"Do what you would like to do, life only happens once, and it is yours to make it what you want it to be – don't think of what I want you to do."*

There are still many things I would like to accomplish – have my own family, live in Africa, not only work as a consultant advising others but also run my own organization

91

– but I am very excited about the path ahead of me and I cannot thank these three women enough. Each so very different yet equally influential in helping to shape my still-evolving path; a graceful ballerina, a committed humanitarian, a patient mother.

I'm still trying to figure out what paths lie ahead of me to 'make a real difference' in this world. Yet, I feel fortunate enough to have these mentors and women in my life who have continuously told me that there is no limit to what I can do, so long as there is a will and passion, and so long as I'm not afraid to make mistakes. Every now and then, I still take the easy path forward with my choices, but I'm hopeful that I will keep these words with me and continue to pursue my dreams.

Maya Horii is a Japanese native who decided at a young age to spread her wings globally. She found the first opportunity to travel abroad at the age of 17 and never looked back. Maya has a penchant for helping and positively impacting the lives of others and is constantly looking for ways to get involved in development work, particularly within Africa. Maya and her husband recently relocated to Washington D.C. so that she can better pursue her dream in international development.

Distant Rainbow

By Deepa Hazrati

A famous Japanese saying goes: "The journey from Kamakura to Kyoto takes twelve days; if you travel for eleven days but stop on the twelve, how can you admire the moon over the capital?"

As Deepa's story tells, life is a journey full of twists and turns, ups and downs. The experience of this journey is what we choose to make of it. Even in the worst of circumstances, and at the lowest point of our despair, there is always that glimmer of hope and path forward that can and often does lead us to a much better place. If only the human spirit persists, if only the heart believes, if we only we dare walk courageously onward, there will be a rainbow on the horizon. It just takes time to emerge. - *Ed*

~ 11 ~

The year was 2009, the month February. I was swept by waves of exhilaration as well as anxiousness as I walked towards the airport. My pace was quick and my stomach fluttered with butterflies. I was about to embark on a new life.

I was on my way to Canada, from India. It was the first time I was traveling alone out of the country. I had been married six months earlier in a traditional Hindu ceremony. "The boy" was in Canada and his family was Indian. As per tradition, I stayed in India with his mother after the wedding until my immigration papers arrived. Thankfully, I got the visa without much ado, and 7 months later was on my way to Canada to join my husband on our new life together.

Like any young new bride, I dreamed of my knight in shining armour - this loving, courageous man in a country where so many of my brethren have headed to live a better life. We can now build the home of our dreams, create a world of love and togetherness, surrounded by friends and a family of our own.

As you can probably already guess, reality, however, was not quite a bed of roses.

*****

As a child, I was shy. Brought up in a typical Indian middle class family, my parents are simple and honest folk. They raised my two siblings and I to be sincere and hard working people. Naturally, my siblings and I emulated their integrity and aspired to lead honest lives. However, our humble home environment did not stop me from dreaming big. Life should be expansive and beautiful, I thought. And, with my parents' constant encouragement, I dreamt about reaching for the moon.

My childhood days were filled with the ordinary activities of a young girl; studying hard, chatting with friends, laughing and nurturing my hopes for the future. Though a weak constitution made it challenging for me to perform well in school, I was undeterred.

When I was twelve years old, my elder sister introduced me to the philosophy of Nichiren Daishonin, a 12th century Japanese Buddhist reformer. While I was too young to really understand the difficult concepts of Buddhism, what attracted me to this faith was reading about personal transformations through a steady focus on what one wants in life, and never just letting "things happen". I can confidently say that this viewpoint played a major role in fundamentally giving direction to my life. I have taken to this philosophy like a fish to water and it has become the cornerstone of everything I do.

One such breakthrough I recall was trying to make it to the top of my school while struggling with my health. I was an above average student, yet refused to let go of the desire to be one of "the best". I still remember that deep sense of joy and satisfaction of being ranked first in my undergraduate college and fourth in the entire university, after years of hard work. That year I was presented with 9 prizes, including the *Girl of the Year* honor for getting the maximum number of awards!

I successfully completed my undergraduate and graduate programs in Environmental Science and made it through the onerous Ph.D. exams required for entry into a prestigious Indian University. I made it to the top three ranks to qualify for a junior research fellowship and University Grants Commission. I was thus eligible for lectureship in the university and, was able to pursue my research with a scholarship.

I lived with the spirit engrained within, that there is a larger world out there and the importance of helping others and self empowerment. As Mahatma Gandhi says – "Be the change you wish to see in the world". Through the regular regimen of praying and perseverance, I was able to juggle the challenges of life. Little did I realize that these small victories were preparing me for the harsher realties that awaited ahead.

*****

Soon after starting my coursework; I got engaged. It was an arranged marriage. Since I was moving to Canada, my professor advised me to continue my studies there. In February 2009, I flew to Canada, leaving behind my family and friends and studies – something I had worked very hard for, all with the hope of realizing a new chapter in my life. I arrived in Canada- happy, innocent and hopeful.

In less than a year, my marriage was over. Or, rather, terminated. All my dreams, hopes and expectations had been dashed. Every single day of those months was humiliating.

When I joined him, I thought I had left behind the torturous 7 months in India that I had spent with his mother, being constantly nagged at and having pretty much everything I did scrutinized and criticized. It was a crazy, disheartening period.

But I was wrong. The time in India had only set the stage for more abuse to come. It was always over small things, like not cooking as well as his mother did or not talking to her enough when she came for an extended visit four months after I had arrived.

When it was difficult to find a reason to fight over something I had done, he attacked me for who I was or, for better put, was not. I was labeled for not looking Canadian enough. My skin too dark and in need of bleaching. Not speaking and walking in the 'Western way'? Whatever the topic of his hatred, the result was a gradual erosion of my very self.

Somewhere along the lines, I realized that he treated me this way because he was struggling with his own identity and his low self-esteem. I fought within, asking why he got married in the first place. Why had he ruined my life? Who gave him the right to do so when he was failing to face the world with his alternate physical choices? Why me? I started to lose strength, with the endless stream of tears and questions.

The combination of being emotionally weakened by his wrath, being away from family and friends in an unfamiliar environment, and having to face the joint insults from him and his mother took a toll. I was over burdened with domestic work, forced to change my looks and, at the same time, pushed out of the house to look for a job. Don't bother dreaming about finishing your studies, they said; you have to bring in your fair share of money. I struggled to adjust, gave my utmost but could not sustain. My health started to suffer.

Faith, family and friends in India kept me going. These are just the initial hiccups of marriage, they comforted. Things will turn for the better, they insisted...and I told myself. It almost looked like they would when his mother left a month later. I continued to struggle to make the marriage work.

One fine evening in November 2009, and nine months after my arrival, he deserted me, walking right out of the house. It was over. Just like that. No words. No farewell.

I was left standing all alone. A cold and lonely road ahead.

My immediate challenge was to find a shelter. With tears in my eyes and a heavy heart, I approached the local social assistance office for some form of support. Deeply appreciative of the precious money they gave me, I was able to afford the dignity of taking care of the basic needs of food and a roof over my head, in the form of a small basement room.

As the days went by, I was able to look more squarely at the situation at hand. I broke down...many times... not because of how he and his mom treated me but because I had been betrayed of innocence, of love, of honesty. It was a bitter hurt.

*****

I was always very fond of the lines written "A marriage is defined not by the mutual admiration two people have when they look into each other's eyes, but rather by the cooperative action they take as they look toward their mutual goals and strive to achieve them". My marriage had shattered those dreams.

However, each time I felt like giving up I would shake it off, telling myself that defeat was not an option; somehow, I have to make it through for my friends, my family and my faith. Through this period, my two siblings gave me unflinching support. I was not able to speak with my parents for a few weeks. I knew that my parents were shattered and did not want to upset them further. Behind the courageous facade, I was overwhelmed with emotions. I leant on my siblings and steadfastly held on to my faith.

I spoke to my mother a few weeks after. The moment I heard her voice, I felt a composed and powerful force urging me to stand up, and not give up. I knew then that there is no insurmountable hardship. I could not talk for long before losing control, but from that moment on I knew I couldn't afford to be defeated. That was the moment I decided to walk this path with grace and determination, and manifested every possible effort to gather myself together.

Fighting him was not important for me; fighting injustice was. He had never looked back, had never asked where or how I was. So what was there to mourn in him? This relationship was a façade. A mockery of a union of any sort.

The big question was "Now what"? Should I go back to my parents? Should I fight him in court? Maybe life would be easier if I packed everything and returned to India quietly?

I did not want to give up and run. So, I took a few decisions. I would not fight him for alimony. I would not turn around and run home. I would look for a job where I was and create a meaningful life on my own terms.

I had to be strict with myself, sometimes lovingly; sometimes upfront. There were times I would feel really lonely so far from my family, yet I continued undeterred. My family wanted to visit me, but I refused. Perhaps because somewhere deep inside, I did not want my parents to live in that cramped basement room and go through the life that I was living. I assured them that all would be fine. They, in turn, picked me up each time I faltered, and made sure that I did not give up and could sail through this period.

I hunkered down and mounted a job search. Within two months, I joined an environmental non-profit organization as an intern. Nine months later, I managed to save enough to move to a studio apartment – my royal castle, where I could have peace of mind. Even if it was only furnished with basic pieces from garage sales, I treasured every bit of it, along with friends who helped me get that far - helped me move, helped me clean the apartment, and gave countless encouraging words.

However, since I still did not have the resources to do more than get the bare bones of my life together, my doctoral studies remained on hold. Given all that I had worked for, this felt like a real loss, even if I knew it would be temporary.

*****

Looking back, it has been a very tough period of my life. I am glad to have been able to find peace and joy amidst the moments of deep despair. I have made new friends - through my faith and from conducting training sessions for newcomers to the job. In some cases, our paths crossed briefly, sleeves touching for a fleeting moment. In others, they linger around, and will likely remain my lifelong comrades. Regardless, all friendships are and will continue to be cherished.

In two years, I have walked a long journey - from the secure hands of my parents to the lonely harsh reality in a foreign land ... from a house filled with feelings of anxiety to the room in the basement where I have fought my fears...and finally to my little abode of refuge which I am decorating with the most beautiful of colours and where I seek to carve out new dreams once again.

Along the road, I have gathered the courage to smile and to laugh again; I have regained my confidence and gotten "me" back. I am stronger... I have decided to use this knowledge as an opportunity to grow as a person and to share my experience as an encouragement to other women who have gone through similar or perhaps, worse situations.

I am reminded of a few short lines from a poem by Dr. Daisaku Ikeda:

Though today may be difficult,
Live it with Joy
Convinced that the road to final Victory
will arrive without fail.

Deepa Hazrati was born and raised in India. She studied Environmental Sciences and completed her M.Phil degree from Jawaharlal Nehru University, Delhi. She moved to Canada in February 2009. Deepa firmly believes in the philosophy of Human Revolution and hopes to contribute in her own way to world peace and the happiness of those around her, through her work and approach to daily life.

Searching for Faith

By Huang Jing

A while back, a friend forwarded me a Youtube video titled 'Binocular Soccer' – where, as the name suggests, teams played or, rather, tried to play soccer while wearing binoculars. Needless to say, the usually agile athletes became unnaturally clumsy. This, in turn, provided much comic relief to the spectators.

Sometimes, all it takes is a small change in the lenses for us to view the world in a completely new perspective. This can happen when we are introduced to a new friend, immersed in a different culture or, simply, when we do a headstand and look at the familiar, everyday world around us upside down. Jing's travels to a faraway place – one so different from what she is used to- brought unexpected clarity to something she was searching for. In reading her prose, I am reminded: Never stop asking. Never stop searching...and amidst all, don't forget to laugh. - *Ed*

~ 12 ~

"Nothing which is true or beautiful or good makes complete sense in any immediate context of history; therefore we must be saved by faith. Nothing that is worth doing can be achieved in a lifetime; therefore we must be saved by hope. Nothing we do, however virtuous, can be accomplished alone; therefore we are saved by love."   *Reinhold Niebuhr*

"Here I come, Dark Continent – an unknown world. Will I be able to find the evidence of faith?"   -

Huang Jing, January 2010

The generation of Chinese born in the 1980s is unique in that they are the first children of the "One Child" policy system. Their formative years saw the first waves of capitalism drowning the belief in communism. Being the center of attention at home – these so-called "post-80s", now young adults, have big egos and plenty of self confidence. Unbounded by religious traditions – the preoccupation tends to be material achievement over spiritual and moral cultivation.

I belong to the post-80s and followed a path typical of my peers – excel academically to get a good job, work hard at a reputable company to obtain a higher salary and gain social standing and strive to accumulate as many assets as possible to secure a comfortable life for the family. I performed very well in the highly competitive environment that I was thrust into – from attending the best university in China to earning a post-graduate degree from a world-renowned institution in Europe and, then, joining a leading global consulting firm.

Despite these early successes, I struggled in my profession, which involved working on complex, long-term issues for which there were no easy solutions. Most times, I was disappointed at being unable to witness immediate impact in the companies we served. Even when project delivery did happen during a relatively short space of time, I was dissatisfied with the direction and pace of it. I ended up frustrated with this seeming inability to bring about effective change quickly.

I came to the realization that *thinking* through interesting issues alone (and being financially comfortable while doing so) could not sustain me in this job going forward. I needed something more to hold on to, something I could rely on, and something that could address the long-standing question in my mind: "What could make life meaningful if life itself is full of expectations and aspirations that can never really be fulfilled?" Religious people carry their faith in the existence of God throughout their lives, facing the sinful world with grace and believing in a better life in the next. What about me? What is my faith?

Upon the expiry of my initial entry-level job contract, I had the opportunity to reconsider career options: to the outside world, the most promising path was to go to business school and rejoin the firm two years later – with more credentials, a higher position, better pay and a clear career trajectory. I was, however, eager to look for answers and resisted the temptation to pursue a predictable future. Instead, I chose to sign up as a volunteer consultant for a cocoa livelihood program in West Africa. I wanted to see how I would respond in an environment without any material incentive. Perhaps, I could find what had been missing in my life?

*****

Ironically, I was more ignorant than fearless in heading for Nigeria; little did I know that it is the largest and probably the most culturally complex country in West Africa, with a reputation for being tough to work in. My introduction to the country was an unlucky one. Just 5 minutes prior to the flight landing in the commercial capital of Lagos, the pilot informed us that he could not touch down as there was another plane taxi-ing on the runway. While these 'near-misses' happen even in the most advanced of airports, this unfortunate welcome did not bode well for my experience in the country during the months ahead. Not long after, I was caught at random roadblocks (in one instance, a group of bandits tried to stop the car with a board of nails in Ibadan), almost hit by a car while walking happily along a busy Lagos street, and told stories of frequent kidnappings (one of my best friends was abducted at gun-point while working in the East).

*****

Notwithstanding, there was plenty of time to focus on what I had come to do.

My terms of reference were to assist local cocoa farmers increase their income through better access to technology, business knowledge and agricultural inputs. In the course of a few weeks doing the field work, I was shocked to learn that instead of re-investing in their land, what most farmers did with their additional income was to 'buy' more wives, have more kids, and acquire cars and houses (most of the cars being second-hand trash imported from the developed world).

Obviously, having more money does not necessarily mean a better quality of life if effort is not made to change people's mindsets and behaviors. Education is thus crucial. But this is a tricky issue as it requires intensive effort and its impact will only be felt with time, sometimes over many generations. As we see elsewhere in the world, such slow-to-show interventions do not favor politicians who are keen on winning the next ballot: for that, the more direct approach of dishing out 'subsidies' – in some places called 't-shirt politics' – to various businesses is more effective and thus also preferred.

I was tasked with creating microfinance products to help farmers gain access to agricultural inputs within a period of five months. But, as the work progressed, I realized that if farmers do not have a credit culture, all risk measures will fall apart. The widely applied collective guarantee approach (for instance, ten farms within a community guaranteeing each other for debt repayment) will also result in collective default.

The solution to this credit culture problem is not in the design of a financial product with a well-structured profit-and-loss statement, but by piloting a simple product amongst a small group of farmers, following up with rigorous tracking and monitoring, and gradually expanding from one group to many. Again, this requires a very long term commitment. A few private companies, including chemical companies and exporters, have been giving farmers credit, and some receiving positive outcomes only after ten years of experimenting. Not surprisingly, I was once more certain that my remit could not be fulfilled within the five month project timeline.

However, the biggest challenge I encountered came from losing trust in people, including those I wanted to help and those I needed help from. I was told lies by seemingly innocent colleagues and counterparts – from house helpers and drivers, to work partners and government officers, and learned that people can be tempted to cheat their family and friends for a pittance. Good intentions were manipulated by the organization I was working for, who cared more about gaining additional funds and accolades from donor agencies than about empowering their staff and volunteers to assist those in real need or, for that matter, having real impact on the lives of the people they were being paid to help. I was terrified and depressed. The thought of leaving the country well before my contract was up crossed my mind many times.

"When facing many aspects of the heart of darkness, in Africa and the world more broadly, remember the light, and we are the symbol of that light." - *email from a friend*

*****

Trevor is a British agronomist in his late 60s, with more than thirty years of experience working in Africa. He leads Adamawa Agricultural Development and Investment Limited (ADDIL), and lives in Yola, a city in the Northeast of Nigeria, in close proximity to the desert. Yola is a place with a very harsh climate and hardly any modern luxuries. However, I was astonished by the way ADDIL functioned. In contrast to many of the staff in my previous organization, every employee at ADDIL, including the secretaries, drivers and cooks, arrived at the office before eight in the morning. Secretaries often worked over the weekends, drivers were eager to take the night shift, and cooks would gladly cater to individual preferences. Drinking water was always replenished on time, the projector was always ready before the meeting and people were always willing to help whenever there was a problem.

"Change starts from very small things, not just in the 2000-hectare hybrid-maize land or the 6-million-dollar-investment chicken farm." Trevor told me, "And you have to be persistent: when I first got here, nothing worked the way it does now; I made things happen—showed people how to do things, and then kept checking as many times as necessary till it was done correctly. It is painful, but you see the change in people, and I believe they can carry these changes home."

I was particularly heartened when, at a birthday celebration for a member of the staff, I overheard Trevor whisper to a guy behind him, *Will you make sure that every driver and guard gets a piece of cake?*" He is a role model, not only because of the smart ideas he has brought to a difficult part of the world, but also for the effort he takes to change the way people work and live. There is no magic for change: just do little things persistently.

*****

Sir Patrick, too, is a legend. He is a Nigerian, and has never lived outside the country. He worked at Novartis Nigeria for several decades, going through several organizational changes within the company, before becoming the CEO of Syngenta (current legal entity of Novartis), the market leader in the agro-chemical business. After retiring from a stellar career, he started PatenGlobal, an agro-chemical distribution company.

The first time we met, he was quite cynical towards NGOs and my motivations for being in Nigeria. I shared with him my struggles and told him that I had come here looking for "Faith". Surprisingly, he appreciated my sincerity and we became good friends.

One day, I asked him why he chose agriculture instead of oil as a career, given that he was from the Delta State, the oil-rich part of the country. He laughed and said: "Young girl, if everyone thought that way, we'd have no hope. My passion is in agriculture, and I believe that I can make a difference by helping the poor gain access to better quality chemicals. Every morning when I wake up, I know what I am striving for. This gives me peace of mind to face the imperfections along the way. I know there are so many problems with this country, but I'm a Nigerian, I will be here for my entire life, and I'm prepared to wait for things to happen."

I was overwhelmed with admiration. Passion and Faith, something that both of these men have, are truly powerful drivers in life. With these, one can move mountains.

*****

The five months period in Nigeria was transitory, and my work seemed trivial compared to all the problems confronting the country. That said, meeting remarkable people like Trevor and Sir Patrick made me realize that however small my effort, it could still make people's lives better. My simple ways of thinking and acting could provide *some* inspiration to others. I taught the house helper of a friend how to make Chinese food, which in turn encouraged her to open a restaurant; gave candid advice to one of my Nigerian friends looking for a job, and he has now started to make real progress; and fell in love with a person working in the country. We gained tremendous emotional support from each other, making each day easier.

In return, I found my faith: By persisting, I can make a difference to people in need through many little efforts – perhaps no giant leaps, but a contribution nonetheless.

And it doesn't need to happen all at once. Nigeria has taught me much about passion, but also persistence and patience.

Huang Jing's life is a tale of multiple cities. Born in Fuzhou, a small city in Southern China, she lived in a military courtyard (Dad worked for the Army), before moving to Shanghai (Fudan University), then London (London School of Economics) for her university degrees. She worked in Beijing and Frankfurt before embarking on her life changing experience in Akure, Nigeria – this 'middle of nowhere' place that helped her find her faith in life. She is now working for Deutsch Bank in China, helping its local partner improve their business performance. She is constantly looking for inspiration and opportunities to contribute to society and remains excited about her personal discovery journey to find the true meaning of life.

Trilogy of Thoughts

By Selina Ho

While working as a temporary member of the staff in a gas station during my school holidays, a man approached and asked if I was ruled by my head or my heart. Random setting, random conversation, random question. Perhaps, not so random after all as I have asked myself the same question over and over for the last twenty years- to rule with my head or my heart?

Selina's triology of day and night; dreams and reality; time and life suggests that the answer lies somewhere in between. One cannot be devoid of the other. They complement and make us whole. - *Ed*

~ 13 ~

Between Day and Night

My soul awakes in the night,
Seized by desires unseen, unknown, unheard,
By the day's eye

Deepest dreams unawares,
Reveals itself in great longing,
In the blackest night

Darkest creatures buried deep,
Rises above the dream-like state,
A specter in the night

109

Memories sublime forgotten,
Reign supreme,
In the cloudless night

A sliver of light slashes the sky,
Dawn breaks,
Chasing away the ghosts of the night

The spirit lifts with the light,
The sun putting colors on the land,
And all seems right

As I lay supine pondering,
I wonder what is real,
The day or the night?

Perhaps the truth lies,
Where the soul and spirit meet,
Between day and night

*****

I fly in my dreams

I fly in my dreams,
a gift that lifts the spirit,
and nourishes the parched soul
The desire to reach the sky dwells deep within
Some say we should fly with wings like eagles,
strong, magnificent and proud,
majestic, effortless
Soaring above all else

Soaring is made easy with love bearing the wings,
when paths are straight and steps are light
but life's loss, pain and sorrows,
weigh on the flesh and spirit

Perhaps....

One should fly like the little sparrow,
light and easy, always levitating,
happy in summer and in winter
joyful and free, wings humming...

The song of the sparrow
the flight of the sparrow
and the life of the sparrow
...small but beautiful

*****

The Wonder of Time

Time is a wondrous thing, I say

It heals all wounds, they say
It encourages, it nourishes, it tolerates

It reveals all things, they say
It permeates, it designates, it cultivates

There is a time for everything, they say
Each in its place, no sooner, no later

Time is fleeting, they say
It comes, it goes, it doesn't stay, seize the day!

A stitch in time saves nine, they say
It prepares, it readies, it prevents

Time is valuable, they say
It is gold, waste not

Time is eternity, they say
It is relentless, with or without us

Time and life walk intimately, I say
As one,
Moving forward, giving hope
A New Year, A New Beginning

Selina Ho was born in Singapore, where she spent most of her life before moving to Washington, D.C., in 2008, to pursue a Ph.D. degree in China Studies at Johns Hopkins University, School of Advanced International Studies. A political scientist, by day Selina writes about and dwells on policy issues. She writes poetry when inspired. To her, poetry is introspective, emotional and necessary, an integral part of life and inseparable from her being.

Precious

By Suzie Walker

"Troubled by men, wrecked by love. Manage your emotions so you don't walk the path that has devastated many a woman before you", an elderly woman advises. We are emotional creatures – that makes us human. But how do we prevent emotions from overwhelming us and pushing us into a downward spiral of despair? From where do we get the strength to manifest our capacity to love and be loved?

This is a heart-wrenching story about a journey through a minefield of men and broken hearts before crossing onto a path of love and God. When one takes pain and turns it into goodness to be sprinkled around in a gentle hello or a deep conversation, or to work with those less fortunate than ourselves in quiet and tireless ways, we can believe that there is a bigger plan and a larger force at play. Pain becomes a privilege bestowed upon us to be turned into something noble. At the heart of Suzie's story is the message that love heals, that we are valuable and worthy of loving ourselves. And, when we do, our capacity to love others becomes infinite. - *Ed*

~ 14 ~

As a little girl, I dreamed of being rescued. I dreamed that someone would come along and gently release the grip of a dark secret that I had held on to very tightly for a long time. I would be protected and the secret would be taken far, far away. My story is about being rescued, being fully restored and being made whole again. It's about experiencing some difficult things in life and, for too long, thinking that "It doesn't matter", that "this is just life!" There are plenty of people who will tell you so. Enough people that you start to believe that whatever you feel doesn't really matter, and also that *you* don't really matter – your opinions, your values, your beliefs – none of these things matter. For too long I settled in the belief that life throws things at you mercilessly and all you can do is to try your best to overcome them and soldier on.

No longer.

Each excruciating event *is* relevant. These things impact what we do next in a deeper and heavier way, distracting and muddying the senses, gnawing away at the soul in ways that appear impossible to heal. Whatever source we draw upon for the strength to recover, we must never ignore pain.

*****

Despite my parents not being Christians, they chose to send me to Anglican boarding schools from the age of seven. They had hoped that the schools would provide me with a good moral foundation. But what developed went beyond that. I started to believe that God existed and that I wanted to be part of his family. This was met with mild disapproval from my parents and a belief that it was just a phase that I would grow out of, like having an imaginary friend.

At my secondary school, my best friend's dad was an army Chaplin and her family lived their lives in a way that showed me how I could get to know God more deeply. I would pray with them and visit their lively church gatherings that were very different from the quiet and reserved Anglican services that I was used to attending. She and I were also members of a Christian youth group. It was with this youth group that I went along to a particularly inspiring talk by students from Cambridge University about the healing power of Jesus. Afterwards, whilst sitting in the corner of a dark, smoky pub, surrounded by fellow under-age drinkers, I suddenly felt able

114

to confide in one of the University students and tell her about a secret that I had been carrying for eight years and never shared with anyone else. I asked her to pray for me. That night was the beginning of a long journey of healing.

It started with having to gather up enough courage to ask my sister if our older brother (seven years my senior, nine years her senior) had ever touched her or made her do things that she didn't want to do. I needed to ask her these questions for two reasons. Firstly, that if he had, I would do what I could to help her, and secondly, because on a fateful day eight years earlier when I had been bold enough to tell my brother "I don't want to do this anymore", he had asked me, "But what am I supposed to do now?" Desperate for him to leave me alone, I blurted "go to my little sister". Awful. He protested that she was too young, and I remember thinking "strange, since she is the age that I was when you first started on me".

My little sister smirked at me in embarrassment (I wanted to slap her). "No, he never touched me", she said. Such a sense of relief. The guilt of volunteering her had haunted me.

I've always maintained that the acts themselves, although horribly unpleasant and bewildering, have had less impact on me than the carrying of the ugly secret itself. But as I write this, I find myself realising that it's not really the case. Both have shaped the way in which I have behaved and valued myself. I had thought that it didn't really matter if bad stuff happened to me physically or mentally and had accepted it – that is just life, right? You just have to march on.

But crappy decisions and choices built on damaging things that happen have a way of piling on top of each other, and the foundations of your life start rotting under the layers of detritus that mounts up.

When I was thirteen, I was teased by my best friend for begging a boy, whom I had been kissing in the bushes outside a school disco, not to undo the belt of my trousers (the boy was a friend of her brother's, which is how she'd found out). After that, I decided that I was going to take control. I wasn't going to be scared of sex. I was going to instigate it. I lost my virginity to a boy whose surname I do not know, in a four poster bed in a castle in Germany. Classy I thought. I was fourteen. I proceeded to sleep with eight others (two of them brothers) until, at the age of twenty, I met the man whom I realised was going to rescue me from this life of promiscuity.

Having severed contact with my best friend and her family three years before, after a major fall out, precipitated by an argument over a boy, I had struggled with my relationship with God and had decided to make my own way in life. And, as if to prove that I didn't need God, here was my new saviour. I fell madly in love with him. I felt completed by him. He made me feel so loved and cherished, so restored. He knew everything about me and accepted me. He was beautiful and strong, intelligent, quick witted and adored by my family. We had the perfect life mapped out ahead of us – everything I'd ever dreamed of.

Then something happened that threw us off course. Our fairy tale wedding was only five months away when I discovered that I was pregnant. I was twenty two. The perfect life I wanted so badly was suddenly under threat. Being pregnant was yet another thing that I couldn't face telling my parents. The stupidity and irresponsibility of it all knocked me out totally. Had I not gone through enough? Was I going to be denied this chance of a perfect life? Something I didn't want happening was happening to me. I considered what I could do faced with this thing beyond my control and looked to my past for an answer.

What was revealed to me was that I should muster enough courage to stop it. In the same way that I had said no to my brother, I could say no to this. My fiancé also didn't want to start a family so young and I was desperate to make him happy. I drowned out the voices of doubt, convincing myself that terminating the pregnancy would put my life back

116

on track and that any deeper feelings I had - a yearning for the baby that was growing inside me, the preciousness of its life - were not worthy of any further thought. It doesn't matter, I convinced myself. It's just a foetus, medically speaking. This is just another hurdle you need to cross before you can have your wonderful life with this amazing man.

Sadly the wonderful life didn't materialise. Our marriage started with me sinking into a depression after the abortion, from which my husband shrunk away from, preferring to sweep the issue under the carpet. I desperately needed to talk about how I felt. I realise now that the shame and guilt that he felt prevented him from being able to talk about it. Both of us were working long hours, he was often away on business during the week. We busied ourselves doing up a two bedroom flat and selling it less than a year later to move up the property ladder. Next we bought a five bedroom house with a garden and started to renovate it. We went on expensive holidays abroad, hosted popular parties and pretended to be happy. After all, we had everything, didn't we?

I longed to have a baby but he kept saying that we couldn't afford to. He had always drunk a lot, particularly with his university friends, but whilst they started settling down and drinking less, he continued to drink as much as he did in his student days. His behaviour became erratic and controlling. He stopped wanting to have sex. Gradually, we became two separate individuals living under the same roof. Nothing I tried pulled him back to me. Eventually I decided to accept the marriage for what it was and stopped trying to change it. It was at that point that he conceded and offered me something he knew that I had wanted. "Let's start a family!" he announced. My response surprised him, "There's no way that I want to bring a baby into this relationship, the way it is." I wanted to be a mother but I also desperately needed a good husband and father for my children. "In any case" I snidely pointed out, "you'd have to sleep with me to make that happen". "It only takes once", he retorted. My heart shriveled and, not for the first time, I felt utterly alone.

He left me three months later. We had the frankest and most open conversation in two years on the day that he left. I couldn't understand why he was leaving just as we'd manage to connect again. But I knew he'd only managed to be so open because he had decided to leave. I was devastated.

I went into work the following Monday and people asked "Nice weekend?" "Not great," I replied, "My husband left me." It was surreal.

A couple of months later, I went to Turkey for a holiday, choosing a tour operator who specialises in boutique hotels in unspoiled, rural parts of the country. It was during that trip that I remembered how I had once wanted to work in the tourism industry. I decided to apply for a job in Turkey with that same holiday company. I got the position and spent two years looking after holiday-makers in a beautiful remote spot down on the south-west coast. I met a Turkish guy who soon became my boyfriend. I felt alive and happy and in the moment. Looking to the future though, things didn't feel quite right. My new boyfriend made it clear that if we were ever to get married, I would have to convert to Islam.

It got me thinking "What would I be converting from?" I realised that it would involve me renouncing Christianity and this threw up all sorts of questions for me. If I felt that I had to renounce Jesus, then surely it meant that I still believed that He existed, and if He existed could I really renounce Him? Even without being able to answer those questions at that time, I left my boyfriend after the tourist season ended and returned to the UK. I settled back into the flat that I had bought after the divorce.

One day, while lamenting over my life with a friend – the lack of fulfillment I felt and how, despite doing all kinds of things that I thought would fill the emptiness, I was still left wondering what it was all about – she suggested that I do The Alpha Course, a ten week programme run by many churches around the world, that helped explore the meaning of life. I agreed, thinking that it would help me answer the questions that had arisen in Turkey.

Three weeks into the course, I found myself writing in my notes "my determination to find God is currently matched by my determination to resist Him". Eventually I realised that I was having to try harder and harder to ignore Jesus, which could only mean that he did exist, he did die for me, he did save me and he loved me and longed to have me back in His family. I realised that I wanted to be fully restored by the power of his forgiveness, mercy and grace and I wanted to discover my true potential in this world – one unhampered by the mistakes I had already made.

Over the years, I've seen five therapists, each with varying degrees of success, but all contributing in some way to where I find myself today. But it's the knowledge of God's unwavering love and goodness that sustains me constantly. He reminds me that I'm precious, so much so that he died for me. I know that he has a plan for me and is guiding me along the path ahead. I've discovered a deep sense of joy which sustains me through periods of unhappiness because I know that he loves me and wants the best for me. I've found perfection that is not possible to find in any human.

As I reflect, I see that I was looking for a Jesus-like perfection in my ex-husband– clearly a bit of a high order! I had really begun to wonder if I was rescuable but it's only through Jesus that I've been renewed, learnt how to forgive, been forgiven, washed clean and restored to be "me" personified. I am free to mourn my childhood, mourn my baby, mourn my marriage. Perhaps one of the most challenging things that I've faced is realising that part of God's plan to heal me would involve waiting until I'm married to have sex again. But since the tally has reached a dizzy 19 men, I think that this is probably wise. I miss sex – it's a whole different language, the touching, the tasting, the intimacy, the excitement, the abandonment - I love it! But I feel precious now and I feel that my body is a gift that I have to offer my husband. Extraordinary really when you think of the appalling treatment it's received.

In spite of this newfound meaning, I am still single. But where that would have previously meant that I would be sleeping around, trying to find love, and getting hurt along the way, I fall back on my faith and trust that the right man is lined up for me and will come along when the time is right.

That's not to say that I don't cry out to God asking him to please, please hurry up and reveal that man to me. I've tried internet dating, had friends set me up on dates, all whilst working in a male dominated environment, but to no avail. However the difference is that I am no longer at the mercy of men. I do not need them to make me feel that I am worthy of being loved. I do not need them to reveal how my life will play out. I am at ease with not really knowing what's in store for me because life is an amazing adventure when you know in your heart, that you are protected, you are worthy, you are precious, and you are always loved.

There's a great liberty in knowing that each day I'm called to transform myself in this knowledge.

I've found a meaning to life, a purpose to serve and to pursue a deeper understanding of my loving God. Right now, that entails doing my part in trying to alleviate poverty; listening, training, encouraging, and facilitating opportunities for people in my local community to transform their lives. My hope is that one day it will also entail being a wife and a mother.

I met a man last week. He complimented me on my toes. They were painted with shiny red polish. He loves the Lord and makes my heart flutter ....

Suzie Walker was born and raised in England. She has lived and worked in Belgium, USA, Turkey, Croatia and more recently in Africa. She enjoys horse riding and is easily drawn into doing anything adventurous. God, family, friends and animals play a large part in her life.

Work-Life? Balance.

By Elizabeth Burden

One of the books of Confucian teachings is the doctrine of the mean – or the concept of the middle path. The goal of the mean is to maintain the state of equilibrium or rather, a perfect balance. Much easier said, of course. Maintaining a work-life balance is one of the topics most commonly discussed in women's groups. We all try. We all end up struggling. Some optimists say they succeed not in a specific point in time, but when viewed over a time horizon- within a lifespan, across different life phases, or on a short term basis – in the course of a year, a season, and for the luckier few - over a month or a week. Indeed, it is much easier to achieve a balanced share of work and play over a longer time space.

I tend to think that even if we do not succeed in finding 'the mean', it is helpful to remain conscious of the importance of balance, and to keep trying so you get it close to balance. Notwithstanding, one should not be so guilt-stricken in the course of the pursuit of 'the mean', that one gets into a frenzy, with remorse over what it could have been. We say, live in the moment and find the balance within. - *Ed*

~ 15 ~

My life changed one night in a dirty ATM booth in New York's Chinatown. I remember getting out of the cab. I remember realizing, as my feet hit the sidewalk, that the cab had still been moving when I opened the door and that I hadn't paid the driver. I remember cradling my phone in one hand, heavy and precious. I remember wrestling with the sticky door to the dingy cash machine cubicle, knowing it would be quieter there than the street. I remember the sound of my mother's voice when she told me she was dying.

When I was young my mother always cleaned our house. I thought at the time it was a measure of pride and independence. In hindsight, I think it was a form of punishment for the fact that she was so smart — top of her class in college, phi beta kappa, graduated an entire year early, but had never, ever worked. I remember how proud she was of all of us — myself, my two sisters and my brother when we got jobs. Her eyes glowed when we worked during the summer. I made coffee at a local café, earning six dollars an hour. "It doesn't matter" my mother said, "a job is a job. It's important to work." And work we did, all of us. We washed cars and fed dogs, we watered plants, babysat, taught riding, sailing, watched houses, stacked hay - anything at all. Mom never asked us to clean up after meals, to vacuum, to do our own laundry — as if teaching us those skills could make us unfit for anything else. "I'm so proud of you." She said, as we trotted off to work at 5am. And particularly to my sisters and I, "You girls are so smart — you can do anything. I could have had a career. I was smart.", and with a smile, "Don't be like me."

Every summer, every winter break, from the sound of the last bell and till the moment our feet hit the bottom step of the graduation platform, we worked. I realized much later that the only times in my life I had not had a job were during my long stints of travel — carrying a backpack from town to town to see every church and climb ever steeple tower, mail postcards and figure out how to book a hostel bed in eight languages. "When are you going to get a job?", my mother asked over the faint echo of the long distance call.

After graduate school I took a job with an energy company and began working as hard as I ever had in my life. When I drove home late at night, the roads empty and foggy, I would call my mother — three time zones behind, and she would say, her voice glowing, "Well, Lizzie, I'm so proud of you." She gathered all of our accomplishments together as if they were hers. I met her friends and they knew every project I'd worked on, every success I'd had, where I had gone to school, how many countries I'd been in. I felt embarrassed but also secretly special to have my career followed by strangers.

I lived out of take-out containers and suitcases. I had mustard in my fridge, and yogurt that had expired two months before. I had one sponge under the sink gathering dust and three microwave-safe plates from *Crate and Barrel*. I went home to sleep, to lug back dry cleaning, to collapse into bed, only to roll up again, startled out of a dream, my Blackberry flickering next to my head.

"You're such a good businesswoman, Lizzie.", said my mother.

On February 22, 2010 my mother was diagnosed with lung cancer, stage four. My world slowly turned upside down.

The doctors told us we had two weeks. Then they decided it was maybe a few months. Or maybe not – no one was sure. Without ever discussing it, we all moved home, my sisters, brother and I, slept together in the living room like we used to do when the power went out -- pulling blankets off the guest beds and piling in front of the fire. Every two hours we all woke up together to bring her medicine. She called us her snow geese – the way, I think, all four of us flooded into her room silently, stepping unerringly over a squeaky board, streaming into the darkness to kneel by her bed. Each person with a job – one with pills, one with morphine, one with water, one with crackers. We didn't need to go together. We shouldn't have gone together. But the doctors told us at any moment she could be gone. We didn't want any one of us to find her gone, alone. Two hours of sleep, the fear, the panic, the quiet breath in the dark, the comfort, two hours of sleep.

Repeat.

My father, meanwhile, was at a loss. My parent's marriage existed almost out of time – a holdover from a different generation, when roles were outlined so starkly that even the language of flexibility had never existed. My father controlled the perimeter. My mother controlled the center. They co-existed for almost 40 years, content in this balance - like spinning disks, always in harmony, never intersecting. Now we had all moved back and the centre of everything – of dinners and laundry and scheduling and life, was upstairs in bed. The balance had inextricably tilted and he didn't know what to do. He paced around the outside of the house. He tried to help. He took over Mom's morning medicine run at 6:00am – learning for the first time in his 37 years of marriage where we kept the tea bags.

He would set up the tray the night before, the tiny china teacup looking ridiculous in his hands, as he set the spoon gingerly into place, always flinching at the clang of spoon on porcelain -- and counting out her medicine as carefully as a child trying to catch a leaf frog, his large hands clumsy with the spill of tiny white pills. I ached for his precision, knowing he believed – we all believed – these strange superstitious things that come with grief – that perhaps a perfect breakfast tray makes some kind of a difference. Perhaps a silver spoon at a 45 degree angle will make her happy. He would leave suddenly in the morning to go to his office. Then return to find all of us working, playing cards, reading to Mom - hesitate in the bedroom doorway, rocking on his toes for a moment before remembering some task outside that he had left undone. He gave the impression of a man leaving more rooms than he entered – wandering lost in our own house.

During the day I tried to work - running down my old checklists of emails to answer, things to do, but I faltered. Even during my worst weeks of work – flipping through slides in the conference room as the sun came up, showering in the locker rooms downstairs before a 9am meeting – I had never been tired like this. Mom slept most of the day, but we could not. As the days went on, she slept more and more – we slept less.

We would dress her in the mornings, a new sweater and lipstick – always lipstick - and she would have a visitor, or the chaplain would come and sit by her bed and read her poems or prayers. We sat with her when there were no visitors, reading to her, telling her stories, asking all the questions we could think of -- unwilling to miss a moment. We brought her all the bright catalogues full of summer fashions and impractical gauzy dresses that existed in some other world where no one was sick and everyone was always five minutes late for a party. Sometimes my sisters and I would go out to buy all the things on the pages she carefully dog-eared, her hands trembling from the medicine. We would never wear them, but they delighted her -- the soft warm colors of summer in her hands.

Even when she slept, we hated to leave the house. I prowled around the first floor, the living room, the library, the kitchen, the dining room, around and around and around, so tired I was dizzy. For the first time in my life, work was not an escape, not a refuge. Not a warm place where I belonged and felt needed. I struggled to try harder, to do better, the pressure of letting down my team at work competing with the pressure of letting down my mother – and eventually work submerged under a long, slow slide into panic. Mom was asleep upstairs. There was nowhere to run.

One day, on one of my endless, aimless laps, I noticed the counter in the kitchen was sticky. I looked under the sink. I remembered Mom doing this when I was younger. There was a bottle of something in there. I pulled that out. *Clorex.* I sprayed it on the counter. Suddenly it smelled like winter evenings when I was young – when the house was warm and sleepy and there was a faint scent of tea from the little porcelain cup and saucer my mother always carried around the house – her cups left on tables and railings, half empty, with the faint impression of lipstick.

I scrubbed all the counter tops. My head felt clearer. I started washing the knobs on the cabinets. I swept the floors. I mopped them with old wax polish from the cleaning closet

I'd never opened in my life except to dig for hidden chocolate chips. The bathrooms were disgusting – all of us living in the house. I cleaned those. I took the dirty towels to the laundry room. There were stains on one of them from coffee. How do you remove coffee stains? I had never asked Mom that. I ran upstairs to check. I suddenly felt, from the bottom of the well of panic, that work couldn't save me from – the tiniest bit better. Righting the house seemed to center something with all of us. Suddenly we all had jobs inside – and at night, to have the kitchen warm and glistening, the beds made, the smell of a fire, gave the impression, however faint, that we could weather the storm.

As my mother got more and more sick, I slowly began to learn all the things she had never taught me. I remembered all the things she loved, lemon scents on antique wood, ironing lavender into a pillow case – crisp and white. Fresh cut strawberries on a plate with a tiny spoonful of honey. How to arrange all the fresh flowers that kept arriving every day, sent by her friends who loved her and whom she was too sick to see. "I always ironed all the pillowcases with lavender, ever since we were married." she confided to me one day, "your father has no idea."

I tried to go back and forth – to maintain my life in Washington, D.C. and to be in Seattle. Back and forth across the country – back and forth eighteen times – no matter where I was, I was always in the wrong place. At work I worried about Mom so much I couldn't concentrate. I called, I texted compulsively. One day in a meeting I was trying to text her and dropped a cup of coffee on the rug just as a conference call began. I pressed the cheap paper towels into the carpet, ashamed to be in this meeting on my knees, cleaning. I sent Mom a text message – another in a series of conversations about carpet stains – tried to make it funny, asking her what to do. For the first time in my entire life, she didn't respond. The next day I got four texts in a row from her – all gibberish. I called my youngest sister. She said, "Mom is frantically trying to text you. She's convinced you need to get a stain out of the carpet." I went home.

In Seattle, I abandoned all pretense of work. My computer was the only thing in the house allowed to gather dust – sitting quietly on the dining room table, plugged in exactly where I left it, its blue light flickering faintly as the battery slowly drained.

On May 27 at 4am, just as the first birds began to sing, my mother died. The rest of that day my family silently scrubbed our house together for the first time in our lives– wiping baseboards, washing counters, folding laundry, mopping floors – trying to stay ahead of the grief. Trying to imagine how pleased she would be to see the house glistening, a calm center in a storm of grief.

Since my mother died, I have not been able to find refuge in work the way I always did. I'm not sure I ever will. My work made my mother so proud. But now, when I look back on those years of 80-hour weeks and business trips, I remember how narrowly my life was focused – surrounded by piles of stacked paper and dust, always more comfortable in my email inbox than in my own life - one step, one task, one presentation ahead of loneliness. I know my mother pushed me to succeed to try to save me from narrowing my horizons – she wanted more for me than to be a housewife – tucked into the tiny orbit of household cleaners and organic vegetables. Strangely enough, I had gone too far the other way – losing myself instead to powerpoint and deadlines. Neglecting friendships, neglecting space for me to be anything else other than being good at my job.

I know how much my mother loved me and how much she wanted me to succeed, but one of the final gifts she gave me – how beautiful and unexpected - was the gift of balance. In the end, she taught me how to make space for myself to grieve - how to build a shelter from the storm instead of merely hiding from it in my work. She also taught me how to remember her. Now the smell of lavender and ripe sweet strawberries, crisp clean ironed sheets and hot black tea, bring my mother back to me —and make me feel as if she could be standing right behind me. She would, I think, be surprised to find that these last things she taught me have been the ones I needed most; talismans against the brutal, the menacing, the unexpected blows of living – a balm for grief and a place to breathe away from the storm.

Now I hope very much, if my mother looks down on me, that she is not disappointed to find out that I'm quite a lot like her after all.

Elizabeth Burden was born in Seattle, but spent most of her formative years on San Juan Island in Washington State. She studied Economics at Smith College, after which she took a position at the Weatherhead Center for International Affairs at Harvard University. Elizabeth has always fought very hard against becoming an author, no doubt a leftover habit from her mother who wanted her to concentrate on making a living. She currently works with the International Finance Corporation on Resource Efficiency, while writing on the side. Elizabeth lives in Washington D.C. with her partner, Rachel.

Worthy of Being an Inspirational Woman?

By Melissa Morris

> It took quite some effort to persuade Melissa to pen a contribution for this book. I had to deploy all the influencing tactics in my repertoire, from leveraging on our friendship ("We need more contributions, please help a pal out!") to using logic to convince ("People will be interested in what a young English woman has to say as we're aiming for a global audience and need representation from your country") and appealing to higher values ("It's all for charity! C'mon, the proceeds will go towards helping someone else.").
>
> Many of the women we approached were like Melissa. They were willing to write, but worried about being inspirational. The good news is that words are powerful. Any story, when told from a personal perspective, can tug unexpectedly at someone's heartstrings. For those amongst us who struggle with stepping out of our comfort zones and venturing into the unknown, Melissa's contribution might just tip you over the balance. - *Ed*

~ 16 ~

I was intimidated when asked to write a piece for a book on 'inspirational women'; others' entries would, I was sure, astound readers with the authors' courage and determination, levels of which I cannot compete with. Could mine be any good? It was worth a shot. After all, nothing ventured...

You see, if one is lucky enough to be born into Great Britain's upper-middle class, it is highly probable that there will be no worries - at least not in terms of money or security. The chances are, however, that one will consequently never be inspirational.

I was born into risk aversion, and there was only one way forward. I was sent to a top British all girls school (away from male distractions), primed to secure a place at a top university, trained to attract job offers from top companies offering top salaries and, after a few years, prepared for entry into a top US business school—all funded by a good employer, of course. By the age of 21, I had two investment banking internships on my CV, a first class honours degree and a position at one of the world's most prestigious management consultancies. Successful, yes, but not in any way inspirational.

I had never *really* sacrificed anything. Yet, inspiring women, or the ones who people remember, have taken risks.

Think of Amelia Earhart, the first woman to fly over the Atlantic. Gutsy, for sure. And a gamble that eventually led to her disappearance, and most likely ended her young life.

Shirin Ebadi, risked her safety fighting so hard for the rights of women, children, and refugees. Iranian authorities have since forced her into exile; these are the same people who confiscated her well deserved Nobel peace prize.

Madonna arrived to the streets of New York with only $35 in her pocket...(or so the story goes...).

These women put something of value to them at stake, be it their well-being, expected position in society, or livelihoods. Whether they succeeded or not is almost irrelevant; it is their bravery that stands out and motivates others to do the same.

And it is these verities that have inspired me to place something at stake. After two decades of predictability, I have decided to step off the treadmill, much to the cacophony of certain family members and colleagues. In fact, I decided in August 2010 that if I am ever going to one day inspire someone (for example, feel worthy of an entry into a book such as this!) I too should learn to step into the unknown.

I have used all the money I have to start a company. Prior to getting my first 'yes', I was rejected countless times by potential seed investors. Presenting my 'great idea' to frowning faces was intolerably disheartening. With money running out, I barely ate one week in order to pay my web developer's wages. That is not something I ever thought I would have to do!

Being (un)fortunate enough to look about 18 years old and not particularly keen on corporate attire, I have struggled with credibility. No longer can I rely on a corporate brand name on my employer's business card to give me authority. I have learned new ways of being heard. The power of repetition works well with an 'all knowing', all-male Board of Directors!

One year on from the day I took the leap, I have had more failures than successes, and still wouldn't say that I am inspirational. But, the ability to recognize those who are is what builds my courage, and drives me to take on incessant challenges. And I have found what I was searching for – a life less mundane than the treadmill.

Melissa Morris, 25 years old and from England, is the CEO and Founder of Network Locum - an online market place where temporary doctors (Locums) can find jobs in General Practitioners' practices, and medical centres, instead of going through an agent. The site goes live in September 2011. Melissa dreams of being a serial entrepreneur and of being inspirational enough to write for the second edition of this book!

Living Love, Loving Life

By Caroline Barrow

Sometimes we want so much to believe that things can be perfect, and that love will conquer all so long as we give it a chance. We wait patiently for our turn, and dance with joy when it comes! We trust our emotions, our judgment, and take a leap of faith. After all, what is life without hope? And what is hope without dreams? The storm of butterflies in our stomachs is incessant, its loud humming crowding out the voice in the head screaming that things are wrong!

For any woman who has lived life by her own rules, strong enough never to surrender without a fight, the biggest risk can be trying too hard. Stubbornly fixing a fairytale that has started to unravel irreparably. Sometimes being strong means not persisting on one 'happily ever tale' and moving on to write a new and perhaps better story. - *Ed*

~ 17 ~

So you're having a long distance relationship. Long distance meaning that you live in one country, England, and your boyfriend of three years lives in another, the USA. It's an 8 hour journey between London and Washington D.C. Even if the jet stream is kind and the flight occasionally doesn't take more than 5 hours, the distance is unbearable. You miss each other, anxious for the next chance to hold, to touch, to feel. But you make do with what technology has to offer, talking several times a day by phone, chatting on *Skype*, 'sexting'.

He is overwhelmed with the attention and love you have shown him. He can't keep his mind off you. Neither can you. You count the days and nights to when you'll see each other next. He drives around with a picture of you in his truck for all to see. Then, one day, he gushes that you are everything he has ever wanted in a woman: a partner, a future wife! This is it for him! At thirty years old, he's had more than his fair share of fun and is ready to settle down. With you.

A single mother in her mid-thirties (yes, five years older), you broke up with your daughter's father before she was born. So you know what it means to work hard and pay your way, balance the demands of a career with childcare, manage expenses. Your "i's" are dotted and "t's" crossed. Above all, you're no-nonsense - like countless generations of West Indian women who have come before you. Your sisters, cousins, aunts have passed on their tales – those-men-dis, those-men-dat, dem-no-good. So, you're not the kind of woman to idolize, to day dream about unbreakable love, to put a man before anything, to fall for a sweet-talker with no substance! But, when you met him some two years before, all the preconceptions changed. You tripped, fell and darn well went spiraling into lala-land. Like a dizzy teenager. Without a doubt. He is the love of your life, and you, his. You're on the verge of an exciting new journey, and it feels like a fairytale.

Back in London, you've been ignoring interest from other men. And that's no easy feat. Without sounding big-headed, you know that you're gorgeous and there is no shortage of attention from the opposite sex. "Hey baby, can I talk to you?" "Damn, girl, you've got beautiful eyes!" "Ummm, could we have a drink one evening after work?" Opportunity abounds to flirt with everyone – from the new joiner in your office to the bobby on the street. Hard as they try, you resist the flattery, the advances, subtle or otherwise. After all, you are preparing yourself for the day when you will be with this man. To move from London – the place you know and home you love - and join him on the other side of the Atlantic. To leave your friends and family. To uproot your young daughter. It's worth it, however. Once you're together, the constellation will be aligned and everything will be perfect!

It takes a year for you to get organized. You change jobs within the company, switching to a more international role to smoothen your career transition. Days are filled with getting the house you own rented out, packing your things, giving bits and bobs away to family and friends, selling valuables on *ebay*. Moving is no easy task, particularly while trying to orchestrate a wedding in Hawaii at the same time.

Planning a wedding is hectic in the best of circumstances. It's even worse when the ceremony is miles away, with you as the only person in the driving seat. Henry asked to let him know where to go and when to turn up. He's not interested in the finer details – neither the girlie stuff nor the costs involved. He's been *laissez-faire* about expenses and mumbled that he'd not contribute. Perhaps, blinded by the excitement of flowers, bridal gowns, hair styles and other wedding frills, you fail to question his motivations (or lack thereof). His only responsibility is to buy the rings (his included). Given that he didn't give you an engagement ring, it is the least he could do.

The big day is fast approaching. Three days beforehand, you have a minor set-back on the immigration papers from the US Embassy. Could this be a sign? Is God trying to convey a message? Maybe. But, not one to give up that easily, especially not where bureaucracy is concerned, you push on. Finally they grant you a fiancée visa for travel to the US with the intent of getting married within 3 months. Success!

A few family and friends made it to Hawaii to celebrate with you. A couple of weeks later, you arrive in Washington D.C. and, despite the excitement, something feels amiss.

Maybe it's the incessant noise from the buses zipping up and down the busy street outside that feels a million decibels louder than your quaint cul-de-sac in the outskirts of London.

Of course, this isn't the biggest of cities, but it is a city nonetheless, and a real change. Or perhaps the dull surroundings of your husband's so-called family home?

Wait, could it be the house?!

Probably over a century old, your new home is badly in need of repairs – from the floor to the roof, the outside porch to the kitchen, and not forgetting the bathroom. The attic is a health hazard; one could literally break a leg trying to manipulate the tiny, jagged stairs. Raccoons that have apparently set up camp in between the roof and the attic walls scuttle around at night, chasing each other to distract from their macabre situation. It'll only be a matter of time before one of them comes crashing through the ceiling!

Downstairs is no better. Every window is cracked, and the poor air conditioner struggles to keep even a small room cool in the unbearable summer heat. Shoes are a must lest you get splinters from the squeaking floorboards. You can literally dim the lights just by plugging in the iron. Not even the rodent stayed; after spotting one casually scuttling across the dining room, you're pretty sure that it left for good.

*****

The house was owned by Henry's mother, but he had lived there for at least 10 years. I soon discovered that my mother-in-law was no easy landlord. We were to fork out $2,000 a month to live there. After an initial sense of shock, I accepted it and even started to fix up the place. Pulling myself together, I got busy with making the surroundings more liveable for my new family – buying curtains, rugs, linens, pictures and new house wares. Henry didn't seem to care. He was happy with the way things were and made no effort to pitch in.

Things went from bad to worse, and not just in the home décor department. Henry's true colours slowly emerged.

For starters, I found out that the gas and electricity were on a 'hook up'. Having always paid my bills, this concept was new to me; in fact, it took a while to fully comprehend that this meant that utilities were supplied through an illegal connection facilitated by a friend of Henry's. Can you believe that, in the capital of the free world, someone could actually connect their house to a power distribution cable, better still a gas network? It is a miracle that they weren't electrocuted in the process. The upside was that, we didn't have a single cold day in winter; the house was always perfectly toasty – all at zero cost. As could be expected, however, the smart set-up only lasted so long. Nine months on, the utilities found out, came knocking at the door and promptly issued a $1,500 fine.

Then there was the issue of what he did for a living. Henry runs a small construction firm together with a very wealthy business partner. I was always told that things were going well with government contracts and word-of-mouth-referrals for everything from odd jobs, to renovations (how ironic, given our own living situation!) and sprucing up a derelict property to turn around a quick profit. What I didn't know was how he really made his money or made up for his short fall when business was bad. Without ever understanding the details, it was enough to know that things weren't kosher.

And it was only a question of time before I discovered his other weaknesses. Henry's former roommate had a key to the basement, and would arrive there unannounced, often before Henry got home, to start an evening of 'smoking'. They sat there for hours, giggling like a couple of teenagers while the stench of weed crept up the stairs, much to my dismay.

I sometimes laugh out loud at how much the place was like *Fawlty Towers*. But the truth of the matter is that it was deeply depressing. Unaware of what was to come, my five year old daughter and I had moved to this, all in the name of love?

*****

137

Alas, there we have it. What you now know is that newly married Henry, young entrepreneur, Mr. Perfect, is a weed-smoking, plain idle man-child, who somehow managed to throw this streetwise Cinderella for a loop. Entrenched in his 'bachelor life', holed-up in a barely liveable bachelor pad, he has no clue what it means to live life by the book, to be married, to be a step-father and to have any measure of maturity in his life. He expresses no intent to learn either.

*****

It's now your first Thanksgiving, the Great American family holiday where giving thanks for all you have means much. Instead of doing so, you dwell on your misfortunes and ask yourself "*What the hell happened, Caroline? How could this go so wrong?*" Over dinner with his family, your ears burn with all the talk of this relatively new migrant family gushing that America is the best place on Earth – most likely because they haven't been anywhere else. You smile and stay sociable; they won't and shouldn't see your confusion, your pain, your anger.

After a few hours of pretence, you take the occasion to become resolute, to double-down with determination to make things right once again. You take a deep breath and commit to making your marriage worth the time, energy, expense and enthusiasm that you gave your courtship. You hold out until Christmas – a month later. You're excited about receiving a gift that says for the first time ever "To my wife..." That anticipation is short lived, however. No card. The present is a sales receipt for fragrance bought online on Christmas Eve.

*****

The New Year arrives. New Year, New Hopes, New Dreams. Perhaps your positive attitude is paying off? Things have suddenly improved, and Henry steps up his game by working extra hard. He tells you that he has planned on retiring at age 35 and has an abundance of government contracts awaiting his business. Things will take off and he plans on moving soon, on buying a house with the cash; only poor people need mortgages, he says. You hold a 9 to 6 job at a large international media company with worldwide reach, but he's determined to be the man of the house. So, he heads off to work early each morning with a confident smile on his face.

It is not long before things start to feel wrong again. Suddenly, you're not sure how long he spends in the house during the day while you're at work, but he's always there before you get back. At some point in time, Henry starts leaving home again late afternoon and is now gone until past midnight coming back in at two, three, four, sometimes five in the morning – creeping in through the basement door and sometimes sleeping there for fear of waking you up. What is going on? Is he working night shifts? Could it be that his contracts required him to work when office buildings are closed? There is a pattern to his comings and goings, and it has nothing to do with the working hours of federal employees.

You look more closely into his personal affairs – telephone calls, paper documents. You listen more closely to what he says as he often forgets things, his stories changing with the wind. Where and whenever he can cover himself, he does. Where he can't, his mother makes up a story for him.

Then it comes out. He has been sleeping with someone more his type; street raised, immature, desperate for attention. She knows that he is married but that's part of the attraction. What is the attraction for him? Who knows? You try to analyze it, to convince yourself that this must be a mistake. I mean, he's messing around with *her*? At some point, your head clears. The 'fix it' approach hits a wall. You understand that there is nothing to mend. You've been blind and things have been broken to a point well beyond repair, beyond what is acceptable. You make up your mind that this marriage is over. You just have to figure out how to and when to leave it whilst ensuring you have everything you need to walk away.

*****

The plans are now in motion to get out of hell and regain your sanity. To refocus and get back to who you were before he crept into your life. Thankfully, this is your specialty. You save some money, secure a job, muster the support of family and friends and find an apartment. You sit tight and wait until your paperwork is intact so that it is safe enough for you to leave. You want no risk that he could destabilize the life that you are building for your daughter. He could cry wolf and jeopardize your immigration process. You execute your plan to leave and are gone from the house within a week. After a six month required waiting period, you file for divorce.

The nights filled with fear, with confusion, and with tears slowly become brighter. Your strength returns. The power that you realize you had given away through an innocent desire to live a dream comes back. You press re-set – focusing on yourself, your family, on maintaining your independence through a career. You're on stable ground again.

*****

Many of us think that perfection exists. I did. He did. Didn't they make us read Snow White and Sleeping Beauty at pre-school? Weren't our bedtime stories all about difficulties overcome and happily ever after? So unfair when you think about it, as reality can be an altogether different matter. Especially when it all starts with a long distance relationship where there is ample room to be taken for a ride in a shining carriage.

As I think about telling this story to my daughter when she is old enough to hear it, the message will not be that there can be no happiness. Rather, Damsel can meet Prince Charming but they may not dance together into the sunset. Sometimes, one of them sees the light and decides that she is worth more than he can give and is better off not necessarily on her own but definitely without him.

Caroline Barrow was born in England to Guyanese parents. She studied Business Management at Thames Valley University, and has worked in account management for over 15 years. She juggles a busy schedule of work and life with single motherhood, somehow managing to exceed sales targets, get her children where they have to be and find time for a girls' night out every few weeks. While Caroline now lives and is raising her two young children in the United States, she still calls London home.

Finds on a Beach: Shells and Stones, a Dead Fish and a Diver

By Lena Brahme

Can the super woman have her cake, cookies and cream and eat them all? A career that provides income and status and also a true sense of contribution; a house with the smell of home cooking meandering through the rooms on a Saturday afternoon; kids who have their runny noses cleaned and all other needs taken care of; friends and family showered with her presence and love; "the romance" with her man fuelled conscientiously, all while keeping her simple makeup and hair in place and adorning fashion that makes a bold statement?

What happens, if in the midst of managing her multiple life-stakeholders, fulfilling roles and responsibilities – and busily stacking up more new to do's in that mental notebook while she sleeps, like a super-efficient back-office – she forgets how she feels and what she wants? Obligations. Expectations. Happiness. Others. Ours. Mine. Very often, we confuse ourselves. Sometimes, we lose our way. Fortunately, we can also find it again. - *Ed*

~ *18* ~

Some time back I chanced upon an episode of the programme 'The Search for Happiness' on Swedish television. It was mentioned in passing that, while Swedes obsess about 'finding themselves', Americans decide 'who they want to be', then, try to achieve it.

I am a 36 year old mother of two, who, amidst a fulfilling life of do's and should's, has somehow lost touch with who she is and what she wants to be.

*****

The summer and fall had been arduous. The loss of my mother, termination of a work contract and move to a new home had left me frayed along the edges. When an old friend suggested in the midst of fall, that we take a long weekend off to the south of Spain during Winter Break, I jumped at the opportunity. Every part of my being was yearning for a time-out from daily chores. January pitched up, surprisingly cold even for the season, and my husband, children and mother-in-law waved me farewell. My four year old daughter said "Mom is travelling to summer". Not quite so, more to spring, it turned out and it was wonderful.

We travelled to the small town of Estepona along the coast and stayed at a hotel that was right on the beach. Temperatures ranged from 12 to 19 degrees centigrade and the weather was ever changing - sun and rain, taking turns. It was tranquil and lazy. We had sleep-ins and late nights with red wine and reminisces. Gradually I felt my pulse coming down.

However, even with the gentle breathing and yoga stretches, a sense of hollowness dwelled within, not too far beneath my skin. It wasn't the longing for my family. I did miss them and actually relished the opportunity of missing them, knowing full well that I would soon see them again.

Rather, the void, I realised, was me missing *me*.

Unknowingly, I have arrived at one of those forks in life, where one has to decide what to do and which way to go. I tried listening to my inner voice for guidance and found, to my dismay, that it had gone silent. What did I want? Not just for my family but also for myself? Who did I want to be? In Sweden these days, what you do and who you are seem to be

143

inextricably interlinked. Being out of employment has somehow made me, in the eyes of others as well as my own, less of a person. So easy and convenient it is to be swept up in a routine where satisfying the demands on the job and meeting the needs of others take precedence over one's own.

*****

I found myself all alone on the stony beach one morning whilst taking a stroll, and started entertaining one of my favourite pastimes - searching for what-not's.

One never knows what one may find swept up on a beach, especially after a long windy night. I walked, head bowed low and slowly worked my way north. Now and again I stopped for a shell or a stone of varying colour or shape - I have never ceased to be fascinated by how these curiosities can have such lustre whilst lying wet on the sand, only to become a dull nondescript grayish white object when placed on a mantelpiece, with the smoothness of its surface barely hinting at its origin. Perhaps, it is an act of cruelty to remove something from its rightful place where it is able to shine in its original glory?

As I strolled along the beach, it suddenly occurred to me that this wasn't just any beach. I was in Spain! Surely I ought to take a moment to hoist in and savour the beauty of the surroundings, and not remain too fixated on what's on the ground?

I raised my head and let my eyes gaze over the waters. The Mediterranean lay perfectly quiet, the sky a husky gray with stripes of radiant white licking the horizon. Somewhere on the other side lay Africa, a broad backbone, sensed but rarely seen. The stillness and beauty at that point in time contrasted vividly and starkly with my every day world. How many times have I allowed beautiful scenes such as these to pass by in oblivion as I rush to complete errands - five, six and seven to-do's in a day – so as to diligently check them off my list?

Pause, look and breathe. Open up to the wider picture and allow oneself to admire and be overwhelmed. I gently reminded myself.

What if instead of walking and scanning the beach sands, I sit down to look at what is around? I asked. Plonking myself on the shore, I hunched forward to hug my knees. The bubbly waterfront interlaced with sticks, seaweed and the odd plastic scrap, shards of building materials and shells combine to look like a carpet rolled out. And then my vision somehow shifted, bellowed out. One, two, three, four... I gasped as I realised that I was perched on a pile of sea shells in various shades, their characteristic ridges and arches removed by the water, rendering them the smooth semblance of the neighbouring pebbles. Hard to see if you weren't looking. There were more. Colourful, big and really, really tiny ones too...I was quiet.

Have I been equally blind to the beauty of my immediate surroundings at home? It is so easy to focus on achieving the goals of the day that the journey becomes a blur. I sighed, looked up at the sea, the sky, the rest of the beach, smiled a little and wondered if there were more lessons to be had on this beach.

*****

Here and there pieces of ceramic tiles could be seen. Being in Andalusia, where floors and walls are customarily clad in beautiful ornamental tiles in homage to the Moorish past, I decided to add pieces of decorated tiles to my list of what-not's to pick. Many pieces I saw were monochrome, having had their vibrant colour eroded by the sun, waves and sand. Only the vivid red ceramic stood out, keeping some of its hue. When we strip ourselves of our outer décor, what remains?

I came to a sudden halt. Having been lost in my thoughts for a while, I nearly walked right over the body of a fish. A dead fish. Must have been left behind when the tide receded. It was large, nearly a meter long, shaped almost like an eel

145

but with a long back fin sweeping like a ridge from its head all the way back to its tail. The mouth ajar, no sharp teeth nor anything scary visible. There was no smell, only the salt-scented sea air. Once a formidable lance in the water, swift and strong, a sea serpent destined to end up in the belly of a bigger fish or as an ingredient in some restaurant's dish of the day, it now lay dead on a stony beach.

I looked around, had anyone else seen it? So ugly, so exposed, so cold... so sad. We'd all end up like that. Be it in a fancy coffin or somewhere altogether different. We'd all die. Did it really matter how or where? Did the dead care? And here perhaps was the lesson of the dead fish: We all die, doesn't really matter how, what matters is how we have *lived*. To the fullest of our abilities or sleep-walking on autopilot, following the routines of every day. Surely *living* is the lesson? So how then to apply this... What am I? I don't know fully who I am or whom I want to be but... I am a mother... and though I am not rooting for the title 'best mother in the world', I will strive to be *the best mother I can be*! And partner, and friend and colleague and person... all to my own best ability. And that surely must be living *my life* to the fullest...

I backed away from the sea creature with as much respect as I could muster, immensely grateful at the trail of thoughts its encounter had steered me towards.

*****

Looking ahead a few hundred meters, I saw an old tower, withered by the centuries. An old light house perhaps? Remnants of a fort? A good place to head back from I decided, and increased my pace. Breakfast had been a bit scanty and a rumble from within reminded me that whilst air, exercise and insights were all well and good as sustenance for the soul, real food also had its place in creation.

As I approached the tower, I saw a lone scuba diver slowly make his way into the water, a bright orange floating contraption in one hand and what looked like a harpoon in the other. Standing thigh high in the water, he let go of the orange floater, revealing a thin chord between the two. Slowly, after having crossed himself repeatedly, the diver kissed his fingertips, leaned back into the water and swam away.

Such solitude. Who did he rely on for safety? The higher powers that be? His own skills and abilities? The odd stroller along the beach? I shuddered at the thought of having to get myself wet in the event the orange floater disappeared below the surface like the ones on a fishing rod. I decided nonetheless to keep one eye on the diver for as long as I was on the beach.

Letting go of control, relying on one's own abilities as well as the gracious assistance of others... all of the above are difficult to do, I thought, but why? Fear? Of failure? I almost stumbled as I realised that as competent, qualified and logical a person I thought of myself to be, I was in many ways letting the fear of failure hamper my existence. Now, how could that be? I looked to the beach but found no answer. I could still see the orange floater in the distance.

Something beckoned from the ground beside me and broke my stride. I hunched low. It looked like the inside of an oyster - mother of pearl gleaming rich and wet. The shell was perfectly round with a rugged and thin vertical edge all around. Gingerly, I picked it up by its side and turned it over. It was the bottom of a metallic can. Something had turned the inside into a feast of beauty whilst the outside merely signalled junk. Yet it was its beautiful inside that had caught my eye, an inside that existed whether I was oblivious to it or not. I gently returned it to its soft perching place. If this old discarded can could regard itself as an oyster full of mother of pearl, why shouldn't I consider myself a treasure, regardless whether anyone took notice?

*****

Rolling back onto my feet and standing up, I caught a full gust of wind blowing straight in the face. In the distance I could see dark clouds rolling in preparing to off load some of its burdens. Not on me I decided, and started to trot back. Just as I was about to reach the point where I'd first joined the beach, I realised that I hadn't seen the fish on my way back. Stopping to look over my shoulder, I couldn't make out any serpent-like shape anywhere along my original path. The ground is uneven and might be blocking my view, I decided. The ground was actually undulating as gently as the water.

I shrugged. A final search for what-not's before heading back to the boardwalk and hotel. Diver... still diving. Good.

A small stone with an almost amberish look caught my eye and I picked it up. As I did, I dropped two shells. At this point both my hands were full of stones and shells and I wondered if I was being gluttonous, trying to gather everything that had caught my fancy.

Maybe I have to sort through my catch and drop one in order to fit in another? Prioritising has never been my strong suit and I laughed as I tried to balance my pirate's booty of sorts more carefully to allow a final acquisition. Maybe that too is an art I need to muster? To learn what to keep and what to discard. To balance it all. To say No every once in a while to requests and offers and Yes to others.

Something clicked. I had agreed to go on this trip to Spain - gratefully, Yes. To the offer of some time out and repose. And that had given me even more in turn.

How often have I declined the things that could have given me new energy? The physical exercises, drawing, hanging out with my friends? In adulthood, time had become such a scarce commodity. Especially time for nurturing the self. I had equated the yearning for such time as being selfish, one of the least likable traits in humans. There'll be plenty of other good times to go around, I tell myself - when the kids are older or when someone else's needs have been catered for.

If they are happy, I am happy... have I carried this axiom to the extreme? If I don't fill the well up every now and again, the well *will* run dry. I must *allow* myself to be happy.

*****

Thank you, I breathed to no one in particular; the beach, the morning, the approaching rainfall. As I raised the little amber-coloured pebble from the ground, a ruffle swept through the drying seaweed around it and there, a jolly neighbour, lay a perfect shard of Moorish mosaic.

Lena Brahme is the daughter of a Zambian Mother and Swedish Father, who grew up steeped in both cultures, though one being much more prevalent than others at different times in her life. Over the years, she has tried to find that oh-so-delicate balance between being an independent woman, a loving partner, a good friend always ready to laugh or comfort (depending on the occasion) and, now, added to the mix, a good mother. An architect, she studied at Lund University and lives with her husband, Lars, and two young daughters, Malou and Smilla in Malmö, Sweden.

The World is Perfect

By Xiao Yu

This contribution reminds me of myself when I was younger – always in for an adventure to try something new, always looking on the bright side of things no matter what happened. No doubt, this is a good attitude and the right attitude to carry through life. Yet many of us are all too easily jaded, losing our youthful zest in the daily tumble. Too often, we let life slip into a trudge and a chore.

Xiao's contribution takes us on a random stroll through a park to remind us of the beauty of our life – no stress, nothing dramatic – surrounding us with ideas and thoughts familiar and comforting, leaving us refreshed to confront the vicissitudes of life. Truly, youth is a function of the state of our mind and not the body. Steer with the rhythm of life, savor its sweetness and do not be afraid to venture into the unknown. - *Ed*

~ 19 ~

My hometown Harbin is a modern city in northern China, close to Japan, Korea and Russia. Audacity, curiosity and adaptability are perhaps traits rooted in the culture of this city and in the blood of its people.

Ten years ago, I had an opportunity to study in South Africa. For a teenager whose longest trip was an overnight train to Beijing, the chance to go out and see the world was just too tempting an opportunity to turn down. So I said Yes, in a moment of impulse, and my journey began, away from everything familiar and into the unknown but fascinating world.

There are many things about the future that I am not sure about and yet I am very much looking forward to them. After all, life for me has already taken several surprising turns - many a time, my predictions and expectations have not turned out the way I thought they would.

*****

One of the surprises was the choice of what degree I should pursue at university - the single biggest occupation of many Asian parents. Like all parents, they want the best for their children – though the 'best' can also be defined in the narrowest possible sense.

When the time came to make my decision, all my dream career choices - computer game programming, anime or movie producer, novel writer – did not pass my parents' reality checklist and were turned down. Instead, they wanted me to pursue a specialized field and asked me to decide between the more lucrative and respectable career options of bio-chemistry, medicine and law. It was at this time that my grandparents stumbled upon a local newspaper article, listing some of the most popular career choices. They picked one and called my parents to convey their preference (though they later admitted that they had little idea what the job entailed; they only thought the title sounded cool). My dad took to the idea and decided it was a good fit. I thus ended up with Actuarial Science as my course of study in university.

Looking back, this is probably one of the best career choices I could have made. I am very happy with the way things have worked out. Perhaps, this is how arranged marriages can and have functioned relatively successfully since time immemorial – someone makes the decision on your behalf based on their understanding of who you are and what you need and more often than not, it turns out to be a reasonably good choice.

My best friend, Qiong who chose to study Chinese Literature and become a professor and writer is equally happy. Sometimes I wonder if my life would have been like hers if that newspaper article did not fall into my grandparents' hands and I had insisted on pursuing my dreams.

Qiong and I have known each other since we were three years' old. We are like sisters, so close that she calls my dad "Dad" too. Till we entered university, our paths had been very similar - we had very good grades and high expectations from everyone we knew. Under family and societal pressures, Qiong enrolled in International Economics and Accounting in one of the best Chinese universities in Shanghai. But in her second year of university, she took up another major in Chinese Literature and graduated with two degrees.

While most of her classmates went searching for their "pot of gold" in multinational companies, Qiong ditched the "big plan" and went on to pursue a Masters, then a Ph.D. in Chinese Literature. Qiong always has a passion for Chinese literature so I was not surprised by her decision. Rather, I was impressed by her courage to pursue what she had always wanted to do. Most people regard writing as an unstable career and very few parents would wish their top-of-the-class and only child to go into that field.

I have no doubt that Qiong will become a highly regarded professor in her field, doing a job she dearly loves and enjoys. But like everything else in life, there is a trade-off. At the moment, Qiong worries about her daily bill, the high rental costs in Shanghai, given her low salary as a teaching assistant.

Like the old saying goes, you win some and lose some – it is difficult to have everything in life. Despite our common interests and achievements, Qiong and I ended up with divergent career paths. She chose to pursue her passions while I heeded family advice and opted for the more practical way forward. The bottom line is, we are both happy and contented with our decisions. What we do not have reminds us of how lucky we are to have what we do have.

*****

Life is not an equation with one single right solution. It's more like a poem, as long as it flows right to you, then it is a good poem, even if it does not make sense to others.

When I was around twenty - an age where one was forming one's view about the world and easily influenced – I met a friend who changed the course of my university life. Minnie is two years older than me and was my statistics tutor. We shared the same boarding school experience, studied the same university degree, had the same drive to be good at what we do, and coincidentally, even shared the same family name.

Minnie and I became good friends very quickly. Even though we stayed in the same city for only a short period of time before she moved back to Hong Kong, I learned a great deal from her. Most importantly, Minnie showed me the impact one person can make and how the action of one can have repercussions on many others.

In my second year of university, I applied for a tutoring position. These positions are normally only open to more senior students, so I was a little surprised when I was accepted. During a conversation later, the professor mentioned that he has an "exceptionally good" tutor who is also a Chinese girl – Minnie. She tutors in many courses and is doing exceptionally well. At that instant, it occurred to me that the reason I had been accepted for the position was probably because of Minnie - the good work she had done, and the positive impression of Chinese students that she had made on the professor. Through her exemplary contributions, Minnie had paved the way forward for me and probably for other Chinese female students too.

This incident made me realize that sometimes one's deeds affect not only oneself but others, including people we may never meet or know, through associations of skin color, race and even nationality. Perhaps, that is the reason why many societies emphasize the concept of the community and a sense of responsibility and obligation beyond the realm of the individual. I have since resolved to do the same for others – to always be considerate of the consequences of my actions and to contribute to make the whole larger than when I first find it.

*****

As depicted by Dickens, life can be dramatic. Three years ago life presented me with both "the worst of times" and "the best of times".

It was a back injury which took me more than three months to recover. I was completely incapacitated and could not drive or work, or even cook. All I could do was stay in bed and watch random movies, getting more and more stressed out and upset over all the important tasks that I was unable to get to.

Life took a turn when I read a quotation, "The world is perfect, you just need to be damaged enough to see it". Strangely enough I started to see the perfections embodied in the world around us – the privilege of being able to walk without pain, the blessing of being able to sit in front of my computer, even the joy of being able to work hard to rush for a deadline.

I started to notice the little things that I had not even thought about before: the love from my family who asked me to return home to China so I could get some good rest, the support from my finance master supervisor who granted me a long leave of absence from work so I need not stress about anything, the kindness of my colleague who gave me rides to the office whenever I absolutely needed to give lectures.

I started to realise that many of the things that I was obsessed with and believed were so important like failing exams and making mistakes at work, were in fact so insignificant in my life. None of them actually matters in the end. What really matters is health, family and friends. What really matters is that I am still alive, I will get better, things will get better, and the world is perfect.

Sadly, as I got better, I started to worry about the "insignificant" things again. In fact, they are not totally insignificant: work, money, achievements. After all, they are what made me who I am. A small thing, perhaps, but as a way of not falling back into taking life for granted, I have designed an opening screen on my cellphone that says "the world is perfect, so am I" - to remind myself to treasure my health, family and friends, to remind myself that things will always get better, and I must appreciate even the smallest daily things that I can do, such as walking and breathing without pain.

*****

Talking about the surprises in life, I am hopeful that there will be many more to come. I would like to travel the world, work in different countries, learn different practices in the actuarial field, and get exposure in all aspects of business. One day I would like to go back to China, maybe build an actuarial consulting firm of my own, and work on education initiatives to grow local talents in fields relating to finance, risk management, investment and insurance. Well, part of me would also like to retire early and go back to writing, painting, drawing, or to become an anime or manga producer.

Who knows what will happen in ten years, twenty years, and beyond? I think despite how much we think it through and plan ahead, we will never fully comprehend the future consequence of the decisions we make today. But as long as we are still alive- the pains, the mistakes and the surprises all make us a better version of ourselves. After all, the world is perfect. We just need to put on the right lenses to see it.

Xiao Yu was born in Harbin in China. She currently lives and works in Johannesburg as an actuary. Although Xiao chose the tried and tested path of actuarial science, she continues to pursue her creative instincts in her spare time. She writes fanfiction, reads and draws manga and harbors plans to retire into the make-believe world in the long term.

Girl Powerful

By Louise Croneborg

The powerpuff girls were a hit with young children not too long ago – sassy, quirky cartoon figures with fabulous taste in clothes, donning their two-toned, three-inch heels with leggings and a t-shirt. With their direct and sometimes brutal approach to defending justice and other beliefs, they became, very quickly, role models for many aspiring young girls. Louise reminds me of a powerpuff girl – maybe the yellow one, maybe the green, I forget their names. Never mind. Dedicated to her work, eyes open wide when she speaks about her latest adventure at a project in Mozambique. Frown-lines on her forehead deepen markedly when she reflects on the frustrations of getting water to people in Lesotho.

But like many of us, she also struggles with finding her place in a work-world where not everyone lives by the same rules, and things are often more serious than need be. Is the answer to go heads-down, conform and get things done without fuss, or to keep what she calls "girl power" alive and take those around her, back to a time when life had fewer qualms and was more fun? - *Ed*

~ 20 ~

Skype rings loud and clear, "*do-do-dong-do*". Those rounded buttons appear, interrupting me from staring into the depths of my laptop. I press green "answer with video" and lean back in my chair feeling a smile creep across my face. A blurry image of a little girl appears. The top of a small face and bright blond messy hair emerges in front of me. The girl's eyes settle just above the edge of the screen, piercing straight at my heart.

Let me introduce her to you: This is Miss Siri, my niece, my goddaughter, my friend and, most importantly, a source of endless love. Siri is four years old and wants to tell me that she is now drawing a mouth on Hello Kitty as someone forgot to give her one and wasn't that rude? I couldn't agree more.

An incomprehensible collection of reports gloomily awaits attention on my laptop. But they cannot come close to competing with the importance of the missing mouth of a cartoon cat. My sister, Ulrica, Siri's mother, pops her head into the video's line of sight, says a quick hello and then interrupts the cat-mouth story; she wants to recount the conversation she had earlier in the day with Siri over a glass of juice.

Siri: "*Mom, do you know that I'm the one who decides at daycare?*"

Mom, looking up: "*Oh really, is that so?*"

Siri, more determined: "*Yes, and Mom, at home... I'm the one who decides.*"

Mom: "*Well, dear Siri... I don't think...*"

Siri, interrupting: "*You see Mom, one day, in the world; I will be the one who decides.*"

I wonder what happens to girl power when we grow up. Why I don't see more of that wonderful force in my women colleagues, my female friends and yes, in myself? That fantastic sense of self-awareness, pride and conviction that I *am* capable of everything and that nothing is impossible. Where did that go? Did it go out of fashion along with rah-rah skirts? The feminine realm seems to trend in and out like nobody's business. We're all trying to keep up.

That girl power - so delightfully encapsulated in Siri's assertion and undeniable in my friends and I as we were growing up; so much so that it seemed to pound along with the beat of my heart. But somewhere and somehow over the past thirty years, the indestructible, don't-mess-with-me, I'm-it girl power just stood up and walked away. Decided that it'd be safer in some distant corner of our inner children. Almost as if frightened into exile as the growing young woman shapes up and sharpens herself to fit into a predefined mould.

Girls realize very early on that there is glory in being glorious, "You look so pretty, you dance so well, you smile so lovely, you are sweeter than honey!". And isn't it wonderful that girls are all that? Oh, I can't tell you how I treasure the moments when my Siri and her sister dance around and sing songs about trolls and snails and lambs.

But the flipside of all the praise is of course that girls realize that if someone tells them they aren't all that – then, what are they? Are they girls at all?

A boy at school once told me that I wasn't as pretty as his *other girlfriend*. He meant no harm! This kid just had lots of ... links in his chain, lots of cookies in his jar, or whatever it's called when men start 'collecting'. Naturally, the only sensible reaction to this judgment was that my girl power came to the rescue and told him straight that there was no way he could say such a stupid thing to *me*!? I gave him a proper smack in the face, turned on my heel, and walked away smiling at the world, knowing full well that he was wrong and that I was clearly amazing.

I'm lying of course. Because, truthfully, girl power never came to my rescue. In reaction to his more-than-jailworthy misdemeanor, my head drooped just a little and I shrugged back in silence with a scar deeper and more painful than I ever would have thought possible.

Girl power was running for the hills.

When we get older, we have to work. The rules of work are invisible and hard to understand. Yet, by default, we adapt and conform so as not to cause disruption. Girls in particular are great at conforming – I have no idea when we learn to conform and how, but we do. Not to say that boys don't. But for some reason women are exceptional at it.

I ask you, why is there so much conforming in the office and so little girl power in the boardroom? And don't get me wrong, I'm not saying we need the Kelis or Lady Gagas to blast into our staff meetings shaking up the discussion on budget allocations. I'm just saying that far too many women that I know have trouble telling the world what they believe in. So very often, we keep quiet to keep face.

A close friend of mine once went to a Life Coach for some guidance. When Life Coaches are good, they provide a sanity-check to attack tribulations that would otherwise have kept you stuck in the middle of a cross-road. My friend was concerned about conforming and the sacrifices she makes when she lets her hard work and professional contributions slip away unnoticed. You know, gets completely trodden on. Reducing herself to a silent worker-bee because she's just like the other team players, helping out in the bigger scheme of things. Haven't we all been there?

My friend reflects: *"I've worked my little ass off on weekends and late evenings to complete a task, a report, an event, an analysis...just so someone else can take all the glory?"*

In response, the Life Coach wisely asks... *"Why do harm to yourself in order to do no harm to others?"*

I want to invent a little bell that gently starts ringing when that happens (ideally chiming Beyoncé's 'Single Ladies'). A reminder to say "Hey, are you gonna let someone shine without you squeezing in to claim some of it, all to keep the office peace? – Coz, overall darling, the result is not peaceful! The result is you going home, glum as a wet cat, feeling decidedly uneasy. Unhappy. Unappreciated. Unloved. Yet you have a choice to make here – you are not powerless.

For me, the realization means that, each day, I try to do three things. I make a choice. I tell the world what I want. And I muster the guts to make it happen. Even if that means falling on my face.

We often think that we are in situations where there are no alternatives. We're stuck, un-free and tied. Whether it's worrying about the status of our pension fund when we should be drifting into blissful sleep, or working at our desks until 9pm on a Friday night when we could be out dancing. Then again, something got us into those situations. We make choices to be there despite doing it on autopilot.

My wish is that when my magic bell rings, there's that split second of exhilarating freedom in our minds that allows for new choices. Say something. Do something. Anything!

When my niece tells her mom that she will rule the world, no one doubts her. There's something about putting words on your choices and dreams that take them half way to materializing to actually happening. It's like closing a door in order to tell the draft to calm down, then opening another door and continuing on your way with the wind in your sails. How else can the world know what you really feel, dream, want and think if you don't express it? And honestly, if you do tell it like it is then there's that chance it might happen. And, even if someone tells you otherwise, it is still worth the try and, for that, I salute you.

In order to make tough choices, and to articulate what it is we want and what it is we don't want, we need to stand our ground. We need to be brave and courageous, and truly believe in our power to achieve our desires. We need to pledge to ourselves and to each other that we will try, even if it is to take the tiniest of steps forward.

And before we know it, Girl Powerful will jump out from hiding, running to catch up with us because this ride is too good to miss.

Louise Croneborg is Swedish, though of the international variety. Born in Stockholm, she has lived, worked and loved in Spain, UK, Pakistan and Sweden. In 2009, she upped sticks and relocated to Washington D.C. She is a Water Resources Management Specialist with the World Bank, focusing on Southern Africa.

Unexpected

By Elena Chong

Some say, life is like a deck of cards. I prefer seeing it as many rounds of poker, with multiple chances to win or lose – sometimes, you are dealt a strong hand, and at other times, a not-so-strong hand. While poker is in large part a game of luck, on balance , everyone has a fair chance of emerging the winner .

Elena has always struck me as a person who leads the perfect life, smart, beautiful, talented. So, I was deeply touched when she shared her story. It was a poker round in which she had been dealt a bad hand. Yet Elena reminded me that there is no need to covet another person's seat at the table because, however it looks from the surface, we will all have our fair share of ups and downs. - *Ed*

~ 21 ~

I often find myself placing my hand
Over my chest with rushed anxiety
Trying to tune out the noise around me
Pushing out the swelling emotion in me
To feel my heart beat against my hand.

I close my eyes and follow its beat
Trying to silence the growing panic
Hoping to hear an even beat
without random pauses or sudden skips
Like the ones I've felt before.

Like the ones that I've felt before
Through my husband's tapping hand
His heavy head on my chest
His other hand gripping mine
Each time my heart skipped a beat or two
Lest a cry of disbelief
May wake the babies who are fast asleep.

Like the ones that I've seen before
Through the monitor above my head
As the numbers shot up rapidly
The nurse's smile turned into a frown
As he rolled in the crash cart by my side
"Just in case" was what he said
With a forced smile on his face
The same expression my husband had
When he told me "things will be fine".

I force out a sigh.

I close my eyes as I lower my hand
That was placed on my beating chest
Breathing deeply as I search my mind
For things to drive out this growing fear.

The softness and warmth of my babies' heads
One on each side of my face.
The unwavering rhythmic beat of my husband's heart
So reassuring to hear in his arms.
The generosity my dear friends have always shown
Whenever I felt helpless and alone.

The breadth of possibilities I have in front of me
As someone who was given a second chance.

I tell myself as I open my eyes
Still blurry from the welling tears
Good and bad things will even out in life
For every unexpected disappointment and fear
There will be unexpected opportunities and joy.

A woman from Korea, in 2009, Elena Chong was diagnosed with a heart disorder, just six days after she gave birth to her twins. Despite the three month long bedrest towards the end of her pregnancy due to pre-term labor signs (not uncommon in twin pregnancy), Elena was blessed to deliver the two healthy babies full-term. Without doubt, bringing newborns home for the first time was one of the most beautiful moments of her life. However, this joy was short-lived when that same night, as she laid in bed, she had difficulty breathing. Telling her husband she probably needed some breathing treatment, she went to the emergency room at 2am, leaving the new borns at home. Little did she know what was coming.

After undergoing a series of tests over 36 hours, the doctors gave her the diagnosis: mitral valve stenosis caused by rheumatic fever. The cardiologist who delivered this news to her by her hospital bed, who also happened to be a mother of young children, ended her sentence with: "it's a miracle... I can't believe you had twins and are still here....it's a miracle....". Four months later, with only a scare or two in between, she went through a successful heart surgery and is being closely monitored. Since then, thanks to her improved heart, she picked up running as an enjoyable form of exercise. Now more mindful of "listening to her heart", Elena balances motherhood while working at a non-profit organization in the education space, and lives with her husband, son, and daughter in San Francisco, California.

Two Lives, One Choice

By Agga Jonak

Perhaps as a sign of the globalized world we live in, there are two contributions in this book about long-distance relationships. Both end up taking risks for love. This contribution is a reflection on difficult decisions yet is a light hearted read of life as an adventure – led one day at a time. This is very much how I see Agga. We met almost a decade ago at a random event for volunteers; there I was, a foreigner sitting alone at a table, when she walked up and just started talking; I remember thinking with a smile that this was decidedly un-Swedish.

Agga is a determined woman, but easy to be with and decidedly natural in almost every interaction, be it a chat with girl friends or, in this case, trying to "figure it all out" with the man she loves. This story is a work in progress and certainly not without complexity. But it is also sufficiently positive to inspire me to look at relationships as a journey that should delight and uplift. And, I'm sure you'll agree, deserving of a happy ending. - *Ed*

~ 🖊 ~

Thoughts from a café in Ipanema

What does a girl do when she falls in love with an amazing man living on the other side of the world? What if this man is five years her junior? And how would the answer be different if he is a gorgeous Brazilian whom she met while on a one month beach and jungle vacation? Does she pack her bags, leave home and chase love? Or does she choose the safer option – fantasize, but stay put in a life laid out along the happy lines of wonderful friends, a loving family, and a society which works perfectly (according to many)? And what if this involves a 30 plus woman, who is a planner, incredibly independent, and not one to follow any man any where?

At the age of three, she had already decided that she would take a big trip around the world, and even thoughtfully asked her Mum to pack a basket of food for her on the road in case she got hungry. She had planned to be away for a while. By the age of seven, she knew that she wanted to have a career that would give her enough money to explore the world, dress like a star and eat well - Italian style? The relationship part, meeting a man and marrying him, came secondary. First create your own stable life, then worry about love.

When she was in first grade, someone asked her class, "So, kids, where will you be in the year 2000 when you are twenty-two years old?" Everybody answered that they would have a family by that time. Her response was, "I'll have a good job and *maybe* a boyfriend". Apart from finding out that university didn't quite end and work-life didn't quite begin at 22, the rest held pretty well; a happy life and maybe...a boyfriend.

Well, she and her Brazilian man tried the long-distance option, traveling across the Atlantic to see each other every few months, talking daily and sending each other cute little emails to share their happiness in between. What are the prospects of doing this forever? Not particularly great. When other couples cry out of anger, or fight face to face, this couple cried when they walked away from each other's arms at the airport, knowing that once again the marvels of technology would replace human touch until they were reunited again.

So finally, after a year-and-a-half of travelling back and forth and kissing the computer screen goodnight, the woman, the planner, i.e, I decided to travel across the thousands of miles of water that separated me from this irresistible love.

Yes, it reads like a cheesy romance novel, but I did it! I decided to go to the tall man in Rio de Janeiro, a man with whom I had, in reality, only spent a brief amount of real time. I sub-let my apartment to a total stranger, which was in itself a big decision. I took time off from work (five months to be exact), effectively putting my career on ice. All to see whether happiness could actually be lived day by day, every day.

So here I am in a café in Ipanema, taking a break from my ordinary life – living and loving in this cidade maravilhosa. The only covered shoes I have are made for the gym. The only jacket a thin denim thing for the odd chilly night. The only trousers a pair of flimsy leggings bought on a trip to Tokyo some years ago. Definitely a world of difference from Sweden in the wardrobe department, where looking tip-top was what I used to strive for -- freshly blown-out hair, impeccable make-up, and clothes that followed the latest trends to a T. Where you would very rarely see me in a t-shirt! Or slippers.

It is different here; my loved ones are not around. Every evening, instead of having a cup of tea at a friend's house to ward off the Southern Swedish damp, I go to the beach with my new pals. Instead of sitting on a friend's balcony in a winter jacket, rubbing my gloves together, covered with a quilt while eating French cheese, drinking wine and watching her smoke, I eat acai berries (yes, they work!) and go to the gym with my boyfriend, cursing that it is too hot to work out in sneakers and wondering how I can do so in flip flops instead.

As it was always in "the plan" to learn a Latin language before entering into the afterlife, I decided to make the most of my time here and take Portuguese classes. I have made progress. 3 months ago I could only order a beer, thank the invariably tanned and toned waiter for it, and ask for the bill. Now I can have a small conversation with the waiter, understand what he is saying about the weather and wish him a great day at work. Most days, I am filled with the happy rush of understanding more and better, other days I am frustrated to see the language written everywhere, to hear people speak it on the bus, in the waiting line at the supermarket and at the gym and yet not be able to comprehend it all. It is not easy to learn a new language at thirty-two. But it is also so much fun.

Thoughts from a beach chair at Copacabana

It is interesting how a person is able to adapt to his or her surroundings so quickly and easily. I found it surprisingly easy to transition from being fairly well put-together on a daily basis – getting dolled up for work, primping a bit before nipping to the supermarket around the corner, and even wearing lipstick to the gym (yes, I am one of those girls) – to being all natural. Except for some mascara on a big occasion. It is a little more strange to go from being all dressed up for work and driving my car along the highway to power walking along the beach and heading to class in my sneakers and toting a backpack. The last time I used a backpack was in the 1980s.

Perhaps the human ability to adjust and adapt is an inbuilt survival instinct? For me, Rio feels so normal now. I don't even think of the business trips with their fancy hotels, nor a paycheck in the mail every month.

My everyday concerns are no longer about how to make a critical telecommunications device project more efficient or how to make that project leverage the series of complicated engineering processes. Instead, my preoccupations are now more trivial and humdrum, yet no less complicated. Which beach to go to after class? What flavor juice to drink under the hot sun? Whether to squirt on an SPF 30 or 50 (when I never used to go beyond an SPF 4). I spend inordinate amounts of time deciding whether or not to wear that adorable purple bikini.

Laughable, you say? True. But still complicated.

Thoughts from my small bedroom in Malmö

Undoubtedly, this is a short break from my real life duties. This sugar coated break was something I needed, something that both of us needed. We had to make a decision and a choice about love. We simply could not continue to live in a dreamland where neither of us knew what each other was like – or up to – on a daily basis. We had to live through "the mundane", like a normal couple. And then decide.

The good news is that reality is great. Those months sharing a small space in a hot country worked out better than expected. Now, more complications. What is the right decision when two people bring each other so much happiness and, yet each also loves their own homes that happen to be 4,000 miles apart ? What makes sense when both people also have their hearts where their family and friends are? Is it fair to say that one person will and should make a "sacrifice" for the other, or is this a word that is too heavy to use in love matters? People I've met here say "Well you will make new friends wherever you move". Maybe, they don't have my friends.

How much do you give to a man who has the kindest of spirits and treats you in ways that you have never been treated before - who makes you laugh until you cry; who makes the best fresh lime juice in the world; who gives you the warmest hugs every morning and has the most beautiful eyes on Earth. What if he were to make this "sacrifice" for me? Would I, as a result, be indebted to him for the rest of my life? Would it just be a matter of time before he came to resent me for it?

On the other hand, could I and should I take that risky step and move to Rio - for good? Hey, it could be great! Living in a city with such beautiful people, cool beaches and electrifying music year round. A city that is, at this point in time, filled with optimism and opportunity. Full of interesting companies, both big and small, and brimming with talented, free-spirited people – an emerging market in so many ways.

Why is the choice not that straightforward? Have I become that engrained in my ways before hitting mid-life? Maybe I am just one of those people who gets way too attached to family and friends for my own good, not able to let them go to create something of my own. Could I accept being "the aunt in Brazil who brings presents home once a year"? Would it hurt if my friends referred to me as "the pal they used to have so much fun with when they were younger, but now only catch up with once in a while by phone"? Or would all this not matter in a few years, when friends start their own families and spend time keeping their heads above water while managing the daily school run in rainy Sweden and looking forward to summer vacations in Thailand with the kids?

I don't want it not to matter. I really don't want to be the always tanned and (maybe someday rubber injected?) aunt from Rio who shows up every second Christmas with Havaiana flip flops in the latest colors for everybody. But if the tall man from Rio asked me to, I could give it a try.

Agnieszka Jonak was born in Poland, but moved with her parents to Malmö in the south of Sweden at the age of five. With her eternal tan, unwavering interest in style, and decade-long fascination with Brazilian Ju Jitsu, many have a hard time believing that Agga is a Computer Engineer, often mistaking her for the happy-go-lucky Team Assistant instead. For 90 percent of the year, she is a Project Manager with SonyEricsson in Lund, traveling the world for business. While she wouldn't dream of leaving Sweden for good despite the winter chill, during her vacation time, Agga scours the globe for lazy palm-trees on beaches that stretch to the horizon, where she is equally at home.

A Delicate Freedom

By Aletta Jones

Freedom and choice. How would you behave if the world in which you live no longer had any rule of law? How would you respond if your actions were no longer subject to pressure and scrutiny? And what would you do if there were no God? In the animal kingdom, infants learn how to behave and co-exist with their ecosystem by role-modeling adults. The elders guide and discipline the young to become happy, healthy and well-adjusted members of society.

Of course, all human societies have some form of law and order. And of course, no matter how big or small the clan, there is some degree of ethics and norms that moderate each member's actions. And for many of us, God exists.

All this notwithstanding, there is still want of one, and ideally more, 'role models' – people we look up to because they inspire and not just discipline us; who appeal to the innate individual side that co-exists with the desire to be part of a family or community; who illuminate the way and help define and differentiate 'the grey' in our lives. – *Ed*

~ 23 ~

To tell you about my life, I must first tell you about my mother. She drove like the devil was on her tail and cooked like an angel. The youngest of five, and the only girl, she left home in the late 1950s to escape a domineering mother who believed that a girl's role in life was to stay by her aging parents' side as a faithful companion, and not much more.

Arriving in London in the 1960s, she wasn't cool or fashionable. I doubt she wore mini-skirts or did drugs like her peers. But she was a strong woman who carved out a successful career behind the scenes in politics.

My mother ascribed a small part of this success to her absolute refusal to learn to type, swearing that any woman who mastered the type-writer in those days was consigned to the typing pool and never heard from again. As a consequence she forbade my sister and I from taking lessons at school. I am to this day at best a two fingered typist.

My mother met my father in 1972 and, having fallen deeply in love with him, married him a short 3 months later. I was born three years later, my sister Alex followed in 1978. My father was 33 years older than Mum, but he was a very successful man, full of wisdom and told the most enchanting stories. So, at first, this age gap did not matter; indeed, it may have been part of the initial attraction. All was wonderful in their cozy little world.

*****

It wasn't until I was six that my father's age began to take a toll on family life. He had been a very fit man in his youth but, as he aged, he went from boundless independence to being incapable of dressing and, at times, even feeding himself. His frustration expressed itself in angry outbursts at the three of us - my mother, sister and I.

His age and infirmness dominated our lives, casting a long shadow over everything. My memory of this time is filled with odd little horrifying moments such as the day my period started, Daddy fell over in the shower and as I ran out of the bathroom exclaiming that I was "bleeding from my bottom" (I was seven years old and as yet the facts of life had not been explained to me), my mother rushed past saying "So is your father" as she ran to call for an ambulance. It wasn't until the next day at school when a girl one year my senior, noticed and explained everything.

As I got older, I began to resent my father's domination. Perhaps sensing that he was losing control of other aspects of his life, he felt a desperate need to keep us close at all times. I think he knew that this behaviour was unreasonable but, rather than tempering it, he tightened his grip, limiting almost every aspect of our lives in such a way that we could not, if this thought ever crossed our minds, find a way to leave him all alone. This started early on, I suppose. Although fiercely independent, my mother had given up work as soon as they married. From then on, he controlled the money; it was his money, so those who benefited from it had to follow his rules.

The rules stated that he must never be left alone; one of us must always be at home with him. He would only permit one shopping trip per week and as my sister loved shopping far more than I did, I usually stayed behind. Some years, I could go for seven or eight months without seeing more than the inside of our house and going to school. We rarely had visitors, even from our extended family. He found putting on an act for them - pretending to be a reasonable, tolerant and even indulgent father rather than the domestic dictator he was – to be a tremendous strain.

Our garden was a fairly large one, about an acre. This was too big and too far from his control. Ideally he wanted to see us, but not hear us. We were expected to play (in complete silence) in the room he was in. Over time, my sister and I became rather accomplished mimes. Twenty years on, we can still convey whole sentences to each other with one look. Our friends find this extremely disconcerting.

Mummy, who had had an almost chocolate box childhood, knew how wrong our lives were and, with the collusion of friends, family and neighbours, she would occasionally get us days out of the house. These days were like sparkling oases in the desert. I didn't understand it at the time, often blaming her for being part of the problem, but I see now that she did what she could to help her girls, and to keep the peace. There was no one to offer her such escapades.

It wasn't until a day very near the end of my father's life that I fully realized that my mother was wholly on our side. Daddy and I were sitting in the living room together; Mum and Alex were out grocery shopping. He woke suddenly, desperate for the lavatory. At this time he was using a walking frame to get about and was fairly slow. Unfortunately his bowels could not wait for him to reach the seat and to speak plainly; he crapped on the lavatory floor.

He immediately began to shout for me. As I ran barefoot past the front door I noticed my mother's pale blue Volvo easing into the garage at the top of the driveway. I halted in the open doorway of the lavatory, the stench was appalling and I felt something soft and warm insinuating itself between my toes, I looked down and was aghast.

My father, whom I now realise was only lashing out in shame began shouting at me to stop dithering and get him cleaned up. The lavatory was a tiny room and, as neither of us was exactly small, I simply could not wedge myself between him and the wall to fix the mess, nor were my arms long enough to reach over him. All the while my mind was screaming "I have shit between my toes, I have shit between my toes".

In his frustration he became increasingly furious, yelling at my floundering dismay. I began to cry. The more he screamed, the harder I sobbed.

It was into this scene that my twelve year old sister walked. She calmly pulled me out of the way and slid in beside him, wiping his bottom, cleaning up the floor and fetching him clean clothes. My mother, who had been a minute or two behind her, found me balancing on my heels (trying not to soil the hall carpet) and watching my sister. I was all but hysterical. As long as I live I will never forget the words my mother uttered when I was eventually calm enough to understand her; "This won't last forever and I will make it up to you."

175

*****

He was dead within the year and I was utterly bereft. He was so much a part of our being that I didn't know how to exist without him. Those last few years of his life had seen his health fluctuate so greatly that, even though I knew everyone died one day, I wasn't a hundred percent sure my father would.

At the same time, his death thrust us into a world of hitherto unthinkable possibilities. We had decisions to make about who we were and what we wanted to be, choices that we were wholly ill-equipped to make.

For almost two decades we had, for all intents and purposes, been his prisoners.

I knew that school would end eventually and, while my friends planned their futures, I didn't imagine for one moment that I would be allowed to go to university. I had never given a moment's thought to what I wanted to do with my life beyond my family and the immediate surroundings of my home.

*****

The journey from my father's death to where and who I am now has been a long and bumpy one. Frankly, you can't emerge from an experience like that without the odd quirk. One of the most noticeable to my friends was my total mistrust and, for some years, hatred of the outdoors. I suppose all those years spent at his side had made me fear the outside world - it was too free and too erratic. I did not know my role in it. The rules were new and elusive, and very different from the controlled but predictable world that I had grown up in.

For years, if there was any chance that I would be outside for a prolonged period of time, I would sit for hours beforehand studying maps of the place, trying diligently to commit to memory any landmark that might help me find the safety of the car or the route home. I was terrified of being lost. I used to write myself reassuring notes and often carried hand drawn maps that I had copied from the atlas or the *A to Z* in my handbag in case I got separated from friends or colleagues.

It wasn't until I was twenty-five that I began to get over this fear. I had acquired a personal trainer at my gym who very quickly grew bored of our daily regime and decided that brisk walks around town might be a better use of our time. I can't tell you with what dread and fear I set off on a walk with him that first day. I was too cowardly to convey that the very idea of walking in an area that I had not studied for hours, made me sick to the stomach. I think he knew there was something wrong, but in the way of all good trainers, he ignored my procrastinations and hesitations and stubbornly persisted. It took a few months of these walks to make me less anxious. As time passed, I began to see that there was in fact no reason to be afraid. I didn't need to be confined to be safe. I'd be fine on my own.

*****

It's too much to say that I am wholly cured. Whilst I no longer loath or fear the outdoors, I still do not understand the impulse to go for a walk. I never need a breath of fresh air, and would happily live out the rest of my life inside the house, never feeling the worse for it. I do realise that I am the odd one out. Occasionally, I take myself out for walks in the grounds of country houses near where I live and wonder to myself if other people around me know that I am play-acting at being normal. I'll eat a little picnic and pretend that this is just how I would spend every sunny day when given the chance.

Inside, however, it's another story. I often feel like a child playing at being a grown-up; wearing her mother's much-too-large high heels and walking about with a face covered in badly applied make-up.

Speaking of mothers, mine made good on her promise. She snuck me out of school to see my favourite rock band, complimented the choice of colour when I dyed my hair blue, and paved the way for me to make my life what it is today; filled with joy, new friendships and, most importantly, a precious freedom.

Aletta Jones was born and raised in the south of England. She studied design, and works for a heritage charity which she adores with every fibre of her being. She is currently obsessed with baking and likes to create fantasies with her cakes, never making the same one twice (unless begged nicely). Aletta has dedicated her life to the pursuit of joy.

On My Own Terms

By Towani Clarke

Someone told me the other day that lifelong careers will be increasingly rare. Rather, our generation can and should look forward to changing professional paths at least three times within a lifetime. It's not necessarily a sign of restlessness. This freedom is a reflection of both opportunities that our parents may not have had, but also of an inner desire to apply our many loves, talents and experiences in different and creative ways.

Towani's story will inspire those amongst us who stand at the cusp of a life change but hesitate to make the move. Perhaps, because we fear letting go of the known – that a dream might turn out to be little more than a flight of fantasy? With thick, dark clouds overhead so hesitant to disperse, Towani chose to pause, search deep inside and ask the questions: "what do I want,...really want,...out of life? how can I begin to live on my terms?" And, true to the origins of her Tumbuka name, the clouds parted, allowing sunlight to shine brightly through, changing everything. Maybe that is the meaning of the phrase: Ask and it shall be granted. Seek and you shall find. - *Ed*

~ 24 ~

I was out numbered, three suited men – Partners – on one side of the room and me, alone, on the other. "We are not asking you to go. Despite the global recession, your job is secure", the Managing Partner reassured me across the boardroom table. "We just want to know whether you are going to renew your contract as Operations Manager," another chipped in.

Four years previously, I had joined the firm as a business consultant to help its rapidly growing operations become more efficient. This first year at the firm was a lifeline in more ways than one. A month before arriving I had walked out of my marriage of 11 years with little more than a suitcase of clothes and two children to educate, feed and raise. The consultancy work kept me sane, taking my mind off the sorry state of my marriage and what I was going to do with the rest of my life.

Towards the end of the year, I was making significantly fewer trips to the bathroom to cry my eyes out - my way of getting over the break up. I counted my blessings for being a woman and therefore being able to cover up the puffy pink eyelids with strategically-applied make-up. Crucially, the work meant I was able to set up a new home for the kids and myself in Lusaka. It was clear from their father's behaviour over the past months that there would be little, if any, financial help coming from him.

After a year, I accepted the full time position as operations manager to implement many of my own proposed systems and effectively head the support side of the business. I loved working there. I looked up to the Managing Partner who had started the business from scratch 10 years before; and had nurtured it to become a nationally and internationally recognised company. Over the last three years, the firm grew by fifty percent. I had mistakenly thought I would grow with it.

Instead, here I was, trying to find a response to the question "Are you going to renew your contract as operations manager?" But what new words could I find that I hadn't already used: "I do want to stay but not doing the exact same job with the same salary"..."I want to progress my career *and* stay here. There are still a number of projects I would like to see through, you see".

No words came from my mouth. The tension built as three pairs of eyes stared at me. No matter how hard I tried to hold them back, tears welled up in my eyes, broke the banks of my lower eyelids and tumbled down my cheeks.

Will anything I say be taken seriously? I thought to myself. It was too late to take the tears back. When I did speak, my voice quivered with emotion. That Friday afternoon I left the office sullen as the depressing truth sunk in – I had put my heart and soul into the job but there will be no future for me here.

*****

In the evening, I sat in front of my altar and chanted my universal mantra – Nam-myoho-renge-kyo. I had become a Buddhist almost 19 years earlier, stumbling across Nichiren Shoshu Buddhism through a friend. This was a religion that made sense to me, was logical and was in line with the laws of physics. The Buddhist Law of cause and effect resonated with Newton's Law - for every action there is an equal and opposite reaction. The equivalent of God was Energy - which was everywhere and in everything, with everybody having an equal part in it. Buddhist practice over the years had helped me through seemingly insurmountable challenges, not least a divorce.

That evening, my chanting was interspersed with outbursts of anger, alternated with sobs of despair. Anger at the Partners for not having had the same vision for the management of the firm or my role in it. Despair, as it dawned on me, that I could not allow myself to plateau and stagnate in my career for another 3 years. I would probably have to leave the place and people I had become attached to.

I kept chanting, working the emotions out of myself, until eventually a calmness came over me. With more chanting the calmness gave way to gratitude. Gratitude to have a well paying job during one of the most difficult times in my life. Gratitude to have worked with a great team of people and to have the challenges of improving the operations of the Firm. Gratitude to the Partners for not meeting my expectations and hence prompting me to think and feel more deeply about what I wanted to do with my professional life. As I continued to chant, things became ever clearer. I realised that, as much as I

181

enjoyed it and was hesitant of making a move into the unknown, this was not what I had envisioned for the future of my professional life.

*****

At heart I knew I was an entrepreneur. Perhaps I was the grandchild who had inherited the entrepreneurial spirit of our fiery, freckled, red headed grandmother. For the year between secondary school and university I had started what became a thriving ice cream making business, delivering delights to several big supermarkets. Unfortunately, the business died when I got married and left the city to stay in a small farming town.

Yet that entrepreneurial drive never really left. Even though I was in the middle of nowhere on the farm, I was always growing or making this or that to sell. I knew that I would never be at peace with myself until I started and grew something on my own. This was after all why I had chosen to do an MBA instead of following my earlier choice of a Masters in Horticulture, which would have led me into academia. I had spent the year after my MBA working on a business plan for my grand food processing idea. I had planned my life around my marriage and the farm. Naturally, everything I did or planned to do had to fit into the paradigm of the farm, including any business I started.

When my marriage collapsed, it felt like the rug had been pulled from right beneath my feet. Without the compass of the farm and the marriage to base my life decisions on, I didn't know which direction to go. There was no choice but to confront the question I had been avoiding for years – What did I really want to do? Not what was convenient to do.

When the clouds cleared from my emotional storm, I started to focus on what I truly wanted and tried to distract myself from the lingering disappointment that the firm had not shared my vision for my role. It was at this point in time that the floodgates opened and my ideas began to flow fast and furious.

*****

New Years' resolutions are an important part of Buddhism and my personal end-of-year-come-beginning-of-year ceremony. In the last days of December, I dusted off a list of resolutions stashed away somewhere in the shelves under my altar. Every now and again I would dare myself to write down a determination that I might have no clue on how to achieve.

For the last two years my resolutions had centered around setting up a clothes brand, Kutowa Designs. I was already designing clothes for my sisters and I, usually from the amazing pieces of African fabric Mum brought back from her travels. Strangers would stop to compliment us on our outfits and ask where we had bought them.

That night, I realised Kutowa was my true business baby - conceived and waiting for the moment to be born. She was waiting for me to believe in her, to give her my time and energy to grow and nurture her.

Then another infant sprang from the shadows and refused to be ignored. Her name was Kuthuta Yoga, Kuthuta in Tumbuka means, "to breath". I had started doing yoga regularly almost a year earlier - mainly because I could do it at home on the sitting room carpet which allowed me to spend more time with the kids. Before long, I was hooked. Each day, the first thing I wanted when I got home was to do my yoga. More than helping me stay fit, yoga was helping me heal.

Six months earlier, my yoga teacher had asked me to be one of the stand-in teachers as she was going away. While I did not attend her classes regularly, I took up her offer, very much encouraged by her faith in me. After several coaching sessions from her, I started teaching classes and was surprised at how much I enjoyed them. Like Kutowa, Kuthuta also wanted me to breathe life into her and train as a yoga teacher.

*****

Never being an either/or person, I couldn't see why there had to be a choice. Do both, Towani! Do both Kutowa and Kuthuta. Did life always have to be this or that, white or black, right or wrong? Besides, I was a product of two worlds, two colours, two cultures – the child of a white European father and a black African mother. A marriage of defiance against the racism and scepticism from both sides: "Why do you want to marry a native? Is it easy to get a divorce over there?" or "We have just gotten independence from the British and now you want to go and marry one! And you choose a broke one?" and on both sides "Think of the children..." Thankfully, there was one voice that blessed the marriage - that of Agogo (grandparent in Tumbuka), my maternal grandmother.

Agogo got her revenge by having fun naming the grandchildren, reminding people of their earlier dissent. In response to the comment "Think of the children" she named me, the first of the four children, "Towani" from the root of the word "Kutowa" meaning "so bright and beautiful you dazzle". Her way of staying, "Don't worry about the children. They will be bright and beautiful" and "As you can see, this union (that you earlier rejected) is also beautiful".

Kutowa Designs had in her DNA some of that defiance and confidence that something beautiful can come through the clash of difference, of contrast, of the merger of divergent worlds. Kuthuta was born from the attempt to handle the stress that usually arises from the clash of two worlds. Like the tension from comments that came from my mum's fellow university students, "She just married him for the money. Just look at her driving his car". Or the confusion, when Mrs. Clarke turned up for the appointment and she wasn't white.

Mum turned to the relaxing breathing exercises of yoga to calm her nerves, ease her insomnia and stop her from snapping at her one ally - Dad. During her pregnancy with me, she did yoga and as a young girl I remember joining her on the sitting room floor trying to contort our bodies to imitate the figures in the book placed in front of us.

At the end of the evening, after conversing mentally and emotionally with Kutowa and Kuthuta, I was ecstatic. I knew that to be true to myself I would have to leave the cushy and secure job at the law firm to give full life to my business babies. I prayed that I would make enough for myself, and my two human babies to live a decent life.

*****

Two years after the life changing revelation, my businesses are growing steadfastly.

Kuthuta Yoga is a little bigger than her sister. In 2009, I trained in Cape Town to be a certified yoga instructor and have been teaching for the last 2 years. In this time Kuthuta has seen almost 200 students pass through the classes and has a slowly but surely growing following, even a Facebook Group following my weekly yoga blogs. Kuthuta is ensuring that me and my, now not so small, children are comfortable.

Kutowa is the smaller sister, though she has it in her stars to shine much brighter. In the last 2 years she has released 5 lines of clothing, has appeared in a couple of local magazines, a local and regional website, and has taken part in four Zambian fashion shows, including representing Zambia at a regional fashion competition and winning the award for Most Creative Designer in the Zambia Fashion & Designers Awards 2011!

It is interesting how one's view of a situation can change. One moment you're in tears, wondering how life could have gone so wrong - How a marriage you based your life on could vaporize; how a job that you so loved and were devoted to could have no room for your further growth. The next minute, you feel immense gratitude for the unmet expectations that had appeared once-so-important but are no longer when viewed in hindsight. To life, for pushing you out of your comfort zone. To the universe, for allowing what comes so naturally to blossom, rather than to remain silent and sheltered in the shadows of your heart.

The pain and loss, the searching and questioning, the late night pondering upon life's next steps has led me to put my destiny in my own hands.

Towani Clarke was born in Zambia to a Zambian Mother and English Father. The eldest of four children, she grew up surrounded by academics and freedom fighters and women's activists. Always the dutiful daughter, she was perhaps expected (or expected of herself) to follow one of these paths. Instead, Towani became a farmer. She has since continued to carve her own path, balancing the many things that matter to her—spirituality through yoga, creativity through fashion design and, of course, motherhood. Towani lives in Lusaka with her two children.

The Choice to be Grateful

By Zeryn Mackwani Sarpangal

This is a book of multiple blessings. From friends, both old and new, who agreed to contribute a piece of themselves when the project was launched. We find blessings in the stories of love and happiness shared and in knowing that one is never alone in times of pain. Embedded in each contribution is the important truth that these stories are personal and unique to the author but also universal in the experiences that many of us have gone through, are going through and may go through at some point in the future. We hope the contributions will touch someone.

Zeryn's story is a wonderful way to conclude this journey. We wanted to end on a positive note, with the first axioms we learn as children –counting our blessings, one by one. In the hustle and bustle of living, it is often easy to overlook the gloves that fit and be distracted by the itch in the little finger. Learning to be grateful take us to the realm of contentment where one can smile and be at peace even when the water in the taps run out, because we remember that the power is still running and we have light in the house. - *Ed*

~ 25 ~

"There is so much about my fate that I cannot control, but other things do fall under the jurisdiction. I can decide how I spend my time, with whom I interact, those I share my body and life and money and energy with. I can select what I read and eat and study. I can choose how I'm going to regard unfortunate circumstances in my life-whether I will see them as curses or opportunities. I can choose my words and the tone of voice in which I speak to others. And most of all, I can choose my thoughts."   *Elizabeth Gilbert*

"Gratitude is the memory of the heart."
                                        Jean Baptiste Massieu

I made an explicit choice a few years ago to say thanks daily. This simple and almost trite practice of being grateful for all aspects of my life has slowly changed the lens with which I see things. It has helped me see beauty in little things throughout the day, appreciate the deeper meaning of everyday occurrences, and seek opportunity in challenges (though not before I have taken a couple of deep breaths).

So here are the types of things on my daily gratitude list.

ℜ A cup of morning coffee – the taste and smell is truly one of the best parts of waking up (though mine is not always *Folgers* – for those who have heard the jingle).

ℜ Quiet contemplation time when I meditate and do some spiritual reading – a ritual that resonates with me and takes into account different religious traditions and reminds me daily that connecting to my inner being in my own authentic way feels better than replicating traditional practices that may be preferred by others.

ℜ The brief opportunity I have to connect with my husband on our daily commute every morning, a routine that ten years ago would have seemed like a far-fetched fairy tale because our union is almost a microcosm of the implicit and explicit tensions that can exist between families of different faiths. And the daily connecting makes me realize the little things that I love about him – the silly way he can make me laugh at a random joke, his determination to make a difference at work, and sometimes even the 'guidance' on how to navigate traffic that makes me try things out of my comfort zone.

ᔈ My commute to work, which I try to make more pleasant (vs. yelling at people in traffic) by a) catching up with my closest friends about anything as small as what was on television last night to something as heavy as what we are insecure about and will need to confront. On a hands-free device, of course, b) mindfully admiring the beautiful scenery peppered along the side of the road such as wild flowers mixed in with cherry blossoms, or c) listening to books on tape, which keep me engaged and intrigued on my ride to work (so much so that I occasionally sit and continue listening to the audio book long after I have reached my destination).

ᔈ The contribution that I can make in my professional role, by being a positive person at work, staying passionate about the cause and constantly putting my best foot forward regardless of the task at hand. It is not always easy to see how a powerpoint presentation or an excel model that I have developed is connected to the broader mission of saving lives through the medicines we are discovering. But I am thankful for the opportunity to do my part.

ᔈ Tiny "setbacks" at work such as water spilling on my computer while I am working on an important deadline; I see that as an opportunity to realize that I was probably taking things too seriously and need to calm down (though getting to that realization generally takes longer!). It also makes me better appreciate my usually handy computer and be thankful for the times that it has functioned seamlessly.

ᔈ Coming home daily to a place that I adore and remains as I had left it in the morning − it has yet to be consumed by fire despite my dangerous attempts at learning how to cook! I do not take for granted the fact that I have a safe roof over my head when I hear about the devastation of people who have lesser means or those suffering from the loss of their homes or loved ones through natural disasters, political situations or other events beyond their control.

🍂 The food I have for dinner because not only does it give me sustenance and energy, it also reminds me how my parents are spoiling my husband and I by sending us home-cooked meals almost on a weekly basis. These meals are akin to receiving love from our families, who communicate their affection by cooking and sharing delights that nourish our bodies and souls.

🍂 The mindless television, music or book that I get to drown myself in at night as a bit of relaxation and play at the end of a busy day.

🍂 My bed, which truly is warm and comforting, especially during cold nights which are not atypical in San Francisco.

🍂 The fact that everyone I care about has been kept safe and secure as we go through our lives and try to make our own contributions for another day.

This daily practice allows me to count my blessings very easily and realize how fortunate I am. It also allows me to get snippets of energy throughout the day so that I have the willpower to tackle the challenges that come my way – either by trying to view them as opportunities or turning to the things that are going well as pillars of support.

It is also a good way to be mindful of the little lessons and adventures that life offers -how I behave in tough situations through a team member with whom I may not see eye to eye; how my stereotype about the homeless is challenged by someone I meet through my volunteering activities; or the realization from the smile of a woman working in our building that sometimes all it takes is a kind word to warm the heart of someone else, however brief the moment, however nameless they may remain.

There have been studies that show that optimism is something that can be learned partially through how we frame situations in our life. I believe this practice of being grateful will allow me to become a more optimistic, patient and mindful person – character traits that I would like to continue developing as my life unfolds in unexpected, but hopefully meaningful, ways.

Zeryn Mackwani is a Pakistani-American brought up in a traditional Muslim family. Against the odds, she married her long time love – an Indian-American from a Hindu family. Her decision epitomizes a wider outlook in life – that everyone has a choice to make good their own lives and pursue happiness and meaning. Zeryn's dream is to serve a purpose larger than self. She is constantly on the go, looking for ways to push the boundaries and to make the world a better and more peaceful place.

About the Editors

Pepukaye Bardouille was born in Dominica, but spent her formative years in Zambia and England. She studied engineering in America and France and earned a doctorate in Energy and Environmental Systems Studies from Lund University in Sweden. Giving in to wanderlust, Pep has worked in Africa, Asia, Europe and the Middle East as both a management consultant and with international development agencies on corporate strategy, energy and sustainable development issues. Her interests are eclectic, but perhaps more than anything, she is happiest simply connecting with people, ideally while collecting random adventures from places near and far with her trusted camera in tow.

Gim Huay Neo was born and raised in Singapore. She studied engineering in Cambridge University and did her MBA in Stanford University, spending close to a decade in public service before becoming an international management consultant. Gim currently lives in Lagos where she is both challenged and enriched by the dynamism and complexities of Nigeria living - with never a dull moment. Eternally grateful for the opportunities that life has provided this "girl next door", the number one item on her bucket list is to give back to life multiple times more than what life has given her.